MASSACRE:
THE STORY
OF
GLENCOE

MAGNUS LINKLATER

PHOTOGRAPHS BY
ANTHONY GASCOIGNE

MASSACRE: THE STORY OF GLENCOE

COLLINS

London and Glasgow

For Veronica

William Collins Sons and Company Limited

First published 1982
© Text Magnus Linklater 1982
© Photographs Anthony Gascoigne 1982

ISBN 0 00 435669 1

Produced by Rock Lambert, 17 Albemarle Street, London W1
Printed in Great Britain by Jolly & Barber Ltd, Rugby

ACKNOWLEDGEMENTS

As a journalist, venturing into the jealously guarded territory of Scottish history, I was grateful for the initial encouragement of Mr John Prebble, whose own book on Glencoe was an inspiration, and whose research on the subject was a constantly daunting challenge. I owe much to Sir Iain Moncreiffe of that Ilk for reading and correcting my text when it was in draft; and to Dr Jean Munro for her information on the Campbells of Glenlyon. Iseabail Macleod of the Scottish National Dictionary, who was responsible for the picture research, also corrected my Gaelic spelling and terminology, and made several helpful suggestions on points of historical detail. Much of my research took place in the National Library of Scotland, where Mr Stanley Simpson was particularly kind. I would also like to thank the staff of the Scottish history department of the Edinburgh public library; the Scottish Record Office; Mr Sidney Easterbrook of the Signet Library; the Central Library, Islington; Miss Barbara Fairweather of the Glencoe and North Lorne Folk Museum; Mr Ross Noble of the Highland Folk Museum, Kingussie; Miss S. Archibald of the West Highland Museum, Fort William; Hamish McInnes of the Mountain Rescue team, Glencoe; the Duke of Argyll and Brigadier Lorne Campbell for a stimulating evening's discussion; Dr John MacInnes; Anthony Holden; and Neal Ascherson. Both Anthony Gascoigne and I owe a particular debt of gratitude to Christina and Bamber Gascoigne, and to Tim Rock and Kathy Lambert, who first conceived the idea for the book and have encouraged us ever since. Finally, it could not have been completed in time without the typing of my secretary Lee Chester and my wife Veronica, who also provided the life-support system that made the whole thing possible.

Magnus Linklater, London and Riemore 1981

CONTENTS

1 ECHOES OF DISTANT VIOLENCE 8

2 STATELINESS AND POVERTY 24

3 'ROOT OUT THE NAME OF CAMPBELL' 42

4 'THE BARBARIAN PRIDE OF A HIGHLAND CHIEF' 56

5 FAIR WORDS AND FALSE TREATIES 64

6 'TO MAUL THEM IN THE LONG COLD NIGHTS' 80

7 'A GREAT WORK OF CHARITY' 100

8 'COLD, COLD THIS NIGHT' 116

9 'AGAINST THE LAWS OF NATURE' 126

EPILOGUE 150

BIBLIOGRAPHY 152

APPENDICES 154

INDEX 157

Opposite: Glencoe looking
west to the Three Sisters

1

ECHOES
OF
DISTANT
VIOLENCE

LONDON, in the early spring of 1692, was thick with rumours of violence and high treason. Talk of a plot to kill or kidnap the Queen spread from the coffee-houses of St James's to Kensington Palace itself, where Queen Mary was warned that a group of dissident officers planned to seize her and remove her forcibly from the throne.

'I was told of dreadful designs against me', she wrote in her journal that March, 'and had reason to believe if their success answered their expectations, my life was certainly at an end.'

There was little public affection for the Dutch King William or his Stuart Queen in this, the third year of their reign. Mary, as she sat alone in her apartments at Kensington, was keenly aware of her isolation. 'I heard daily . . . that the King and I were less loved, that we had many enemies and less friends', she wrote.

As royal popularity waned, so confidence grew among the enemies of the King. In Jacobite circles, it was common talk that Mary's father, James II, was about to return to England and reclaim his throne. Since the New Year, a French army of 20,000 men had been poised on the Cherbourg peninsula, waiting only for James to join them from Paris and launch an invasion. The exiled king had been assured that England was now a divided and discontented nation. Even the Admiral of the Fleet, the cautious William Russell, was said to be harbouring thoughts of loyalty to the Jacobite cause.

Government reprisals were inevitable. Suspects in London – Papists and Jacobites – were rounded up or ordered to leave the city, and, amid suspicion on both sides, propaganda became a powerful weapon. A document signed by James, which gave warning of the revenge he planned for his opponents, was circulated to blacken his reputation. Another, hastily substituted by his supporters, suggested that the first was a fabrication.

One man well removed from these scenes of intrigue was King William himself. He was, as usual for the time of year, in Flanders, pursuing his long campaign against Louis XIV's army across the river Meuse. He had left London in early March after a wretched winter spent struggling with asthmatic attacks. On one occasion he had frightened the Queen by coughing blood for a whole day and a night. 'His life seems to hang by a thread', observed the Duke of Savoy's ambassador.

But William was tough enough. He had attended the great ball that he and the Queen had thrown on Twelfth Night at Kensington Palace, and had lost £100 at the gaming tables afterwards. Next day he had gone, *incognito*, to the House of Lords, to observe the Duke of Norfolk suing some scoundrel for enticing his Duchess.

What had really concerned William, however, was Flanders and the difficult campaign which loomed ahead. Before his departure, he set about clearing up matters which needed his attention. He held meetings with his advisers, the Earls of Romney, Nottingham and Portland; he discussed four new pavilions planned for Kensington Palace with his architect, Christopher Wren; and he learned from the Marquis of Caermarthen that at long last Parliament had voted him most of the supplies he needed for his army of 65,000 men.

Above: James II, 'irresolute monarch-in-exile'
By Sir Peter Lely, *c* 1665–70

Above right: Mary II in 1685. 'I heard daily that the King and I were less loved . . .'
By an unknown artist, adapted from William Wissing

Opposite: William III. 'He understood continental politics thoroughly and gave his whole mind to them. To English business he attended less, and to Scotch business least of all'
After Sir Peter Lely, 1677

In the middle of all this, he received his Secretary of State for Scotland, Sir John Dalrymple, the Master of Stair, and, on 11th and 16th January he signed two sets of documents relating to the Highlands of Scotland.

Then on 4th March he was off, leaving promptly at 4 am to join his camp in Flanders. There is no hint that Scottish matters weighed heavily or, indeed, at all on the regal conscience. 'The truth is', noted Macaulay, 'that the King understood continental politics thoroughly and gave his whole mind to them. To English business he attended less, and to Scotch business least of all.' But in this case the Scotch business concerned a matter of life and death. When word of it reached London that April, six weeks after William's departure, it was instantly taken up by his enemies and used as a weapon against him.

The rumour surfaced first in the *Paris Gazette*, a Jacobite propaganda sheet printed in France and circulated among supporters of James II. Its usual fare was an indignant blend of religion and politics, fulminations against King William's Protestantism, and

complaints about repression of the true faith. On this occasion it contained a brief account of murder in the Highlands – in a place called Glencoe.

The Laird of Glencoe, reported the *Gazette*, had been 'butchered', along with many of his clan, by soldiers of the Earl of Argyll's regiment. Some 200 other inhabitants had escaped. Realising the 'horror of so barbarous an action', those concerned had put about a rumour that the Laird had actually been killed in an ambush with his weapons in his hand. But that was not true, said the *Gazette*, and the lie served to show 'what little trust can be placed on the words of those who rule'.

To those who read this account in London, it must have seemed a remote affair. As far as most Englishmen were aware, there was usually trouble of some kind among the wilder Highland clans, and if the army had had to use force, it was probably no more than they deserved. That view would have been echoed fervently by a good many people north of the border as well; when William was offered the crown of Scotland in 1689, his Scottish subjects had petitioned him to take 'an effectual course to repress the depredations of the Highland Clans'.

Since then the Highlands had been relatively quiet. To all except those most intimately involved, the Glencoe matter appeared to be a minor, if bloody, regression, and in May it was swamped by more immediate news. As the English fleet prepared to sail against the French, a group of Jacobite officers was arrested for plotting to seize 'the Queen's person', and thrown into prison. Mary felt sufficiently relieved to venture out in public and inspect her troops in Hyde Park, and Admiral Russell, swearing total loyalty to the Queen, joined up with the Dutch fleet at Spithead and proceeded to rout the French off Cherbourg. It was a famous victory and a cause for national jubilation.

One man, however, detected more in this Glencoe affair than the echoes of distant violence. Charles Leslie was an Irish-born Catholic, son of a bishop, cleric, sometime barrister, polemicist, and deep-dyed opponent of William's Government. He was a 'nonjuror' – one of the several hundred clergymen who had refused to change their oaths of loyalty from James II to William and Mary, as required by Act of Parliament – and he had been deprived of his Irish curacy as a result. Now living in London, he had transferred his energies to turning out an astonishing number of pamphlets, most of them concerned with Ireland, all of them dissecting the religious and political ideas of the day with powerful and obstinate conviction. 'Leslie was a reasoner not to be reasoned against', wrote an admiring Samuel Johnson in later years.

Leslie possessed the instincts of a journalist. He was indefatigable in his search for firm evidence to back up his arguments, and he liked to direct his readers with some force towards the right questions. The Declaration of Rights, read by the Parliament of England to William and Mary on their accession, and passed as a Bill of Rights in December 1689, contained, in written form, some basic expression of liberty, both for Parliament and for the individual. It prohibited the use of 'cruel and unusual punishment' against the ordinary citizen, and for the first time it set limitations on the power of the King to use an army 'within the kingdom in time of peace'. On both counts, the Glencoe murders seemed to represent a glaring abuse of power and of principle.

As far as Leslie could discover, responsibility for the Glencoe business seemed to lie higher up than with a group of apparently brutal soldiers. He therefore set about collecting the facts by sending for more information from Jacobite circles in Scotland. It soon became clear that north of the border Glencoe had already become a *cause célèbre*.

Since August of the previous year, the question of whether the more unruly Highland clans would come forward to take the oath of allegiance to William and Mary had been eagerly discussed. Proclamations requiring all those who had taken up arms against the King to come forward and swear loyalty had been fixed to market crosses in towns throughout Scotland, and the Privy Council in Edinburgh had given them until 31st December 1691 to sign. As the deadline approached, rumours spread that several had held out and refused to swear the oath.

By the end of February 1692, a story reached Edinburgh that there had been some sort of action against one of the Lochaber clans in the west. At first it sounded as if there had been a clan battle – a night raid by Campbells on one of their MacDonald enemies. But it soon became clear that if any Campbells had been involved, then they had been in uniform. Government troops, said those who knew, had taken part in a harsh military reprisal.

When, a month later, officers and men of the Earl of Argyll's regiment passed through Edinburgh *en route* to the campaign in Flanders, they were able to flesh out the bare rumour of what had actually taken place in Glencoe in the early morning of Saturday, 13th February.

This was the story that reached Charles Leslie in London. Even more important to him were copies of two documents which also arrived from Scotland. They were military orders, signed by officers and marked 'For Their Majesties' Service'; they contained proof that whatever had happened in Glencoe that day had been carefully planned and premeditated. They set out, in chilling detail, instructions for the elimination of an entire community.

By late April, Leslie's account was ready. He knew, however, that publication of such contentious material was dangerous. Although the reign of William and Mary was to see the birth of English journalism, with scores of newspapers springing up to usher in the age of Addison, Steele, Defoe and Swift, heavy censorship was still in force in 1692 and would not be abolished until the following year. To publish an attack on the Government was to render both author and printer liable to imprisonment. So Leslie took the precaution of slipping the Glencoe story into a weighty pamphlet on a quite unrelated subject – the religious question in Ireland – and he wrote it in the form of a letter from an anonymous 'Gentleman in Edinburgh'. Few who purchased it would have suspected the revelation it contained. But it was at least published; Glencoe was now firmly in the public domain.

Leslie, at this stage, attempted no explanation for the clinical brutality he claimed had taken place, but he took care to sow the

14

Above: John Campbell, first Earl of Breadalbane – 'cunning as a fox, wise as a serpent, slippery as an eel' By Sir John de Medina

Left: Archibald Campbell, tenth Earl and first Duke of Argyll – an 'hereditary capacity for aggrandisement like the Hapsburgs or the Brandenburgs' By Nicholas Maes, 1701

Opposite: John Dalrymple, Master of Stair, second Viscount Stair, and first Earl of Stair – 'the slippery Stair goes unstraight' By Sir John de Medina

Below: Robert Campbell of Glenlyon – 'an object of compassion when I see him' By an unknown artist

implications of the story in his readers' minds. 'You say there are many in England who cannot believe such a thing could be done and publick Justice not executed upon the ruffians', he wrote, 'for they take it for granted that no such order could be given by the Government'.

But could it? Leslie left the question open. 'But as to the matter of fact of the murder of Glencoe', he concluded, 'you may depend upon it as certain and undeniable'.

First reactions to such seditious talk were predictable. Leslie's pamphlet was dismissed as 'Jacobite mendacity', and attempts were made to trace the author. But already those directly connected with the affair had begun, either by silence or by bluster, to confirm the skeleton of his case in the several ways open to men who are either guilty or narrowly innocent.

The officer in charge, Captain Robert Campbell of Glenlyon – at 60, curiously old for so junior a command – was defiant. He announced openly in the Royal Coffee House in Edinburgh that he had nothing to be ashamed of.

Colonel John Hill, the elderly and long-serving commander of the garrison at Fort William, seemed apprehensive. 'I understand that there are some severe reflections upon the action in Glencoe, and that perhaps by good men too', he wrote.

Sir Thomas Livingstone, Commander-in-Chief, at the age of 40, of the King's forces in Scotland, reacted like all military men wearied by the influence of outsiders on a soldier's business. All that had taken place was a simple military action. He saw no reason why civilians, and above all politicians, should interfere.

But it was beyond this clear military chain of command that final responsibility lay. Leslie may have been aware that other names were being mentioned in connection with the Glencoe affair, but he would not have dared, at this stage, to publish them. They were the names of men whose rank and standing in the country were awesome, and the evidence against them so far was tenuous. Nevertheless, in private, these men too began quietly to distance themselves from the events.

Some weeks after the action, a messenger arrived in Appin on the west coast of Argyll, where many of the fleeing men had taken refuge. He came on behalf of one of the most powerful lairds in Scotland – Sir John Campbell, Laird of Glenorchy, Earl of Breadalbane, known to his clansmen as 'Grey John'. Breadalbane, the emissary said, had a proposal to make: if the MacDonalds would testify that he was innocent of the slaughter, then he would do his best to help them. Breadalbane's mission suggested that here was a man whose conscience was far from clear.

Then there was another Campbell, even more powerful: Archibald, tenth Earl of Argyll, Chief of Clan Campbell and Colonel of the Argyll Regiment, which he himself had raised, and whose soldiers had been in Glencoe. This connection brought the matter close to the royal household, for Argyll had been with William in Holland before his accession, and had accompanied him to England in 1688, one of three men who had offered him the crown of Scotland. He too knew something of the matter, though he professed a lofty detachment.

Finally, there was the King's Minister: Sir John Dalrymple, Master of Stair, William III's Secretary of State for Scotland. He too was close to the King, and was the second of the three men who had offered him the Scottish crown. But he was far from detached. 'When you are right, fear no one . . .', he wrote to Colonel Hill that April. 'All I regret is that any of [them] got away . . .' Having penned these abrupt thoughts, he left to join his King in Flanders, and for the next three years was to be the only official conduit for the King's own views on the subject.

As for William himself, he had other things on his mind. He was in the middle of the most disastrous summer of his Flanders campaign. In May he had lost the 'impregnable' fortress of Namur to Louis XIV's victorious army, and two months later he was to watch the terrible defeat of his forces at Steinkirk, where his English and Scottish battalions alike were cut to pieces, leaving 6,000 dead on the field and William in tears.

But Glencoe would return to haunt him. As Leslie pointed out, what had happened there was an affront which demanded that 'publick justice be executed upon the ruffians' who were responsible. Whether William himself should be numbered among them remained to be seen.

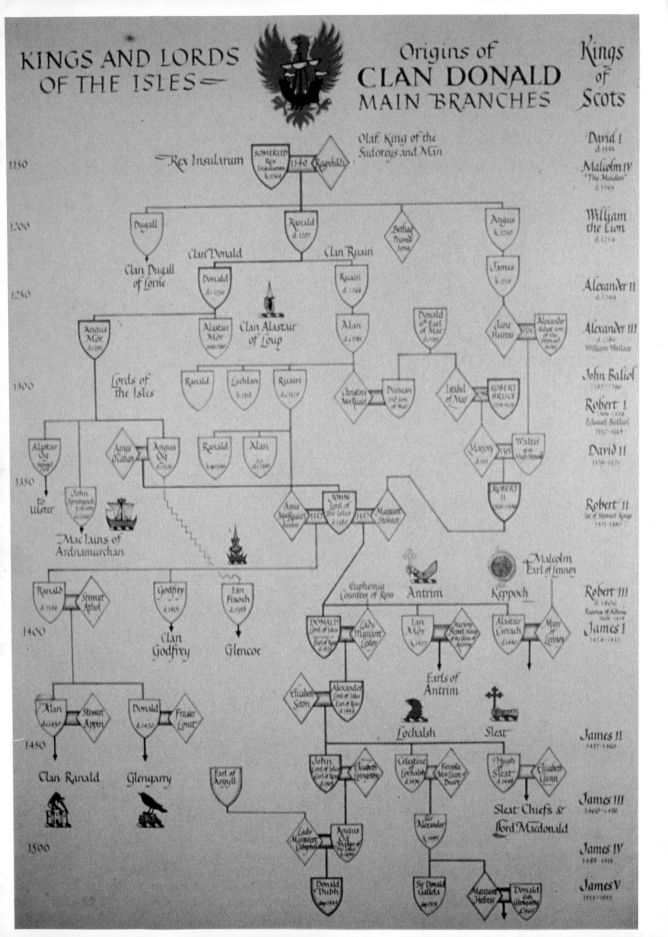

Far left: The Lords of the Isles and their descendants, the MacDonalds

Left: The genealogical tree of the Glenorchy Campbells By George Jamesone

Overleaf: 'The symbol of their fierce and continuing independence' – Glencoe looking east

19

Glencoe in its setting

Devil's Staircase

Altnafeadh

Kinlochleven

Meeting of the
Three Waters

THI

Achtriochtan

THREE

Loch
Achtriochtan

River Coe

AONACH EAGACH

Pap of Glencoe

Signal
Rock

Leacantuim

Meall Mc

Achnacon

Carnoch

Inverrigan

Invercoe

LOCH LEVEN

Black Mount

Rannoch Moor

GLEN ETIVE

BUACHAILLE ETIVE MÓR

River Etive

BUACHAILLE ETIVE BEAG

Beinn Fhada

Coire Gabhail

Geàrr Aonach

Dalness

Aonach Dubh

Bidean nam Bian

SISTERS

MacIain's summer house

Gleann-leac-na-muidhe

N

2

STATELINESS
AND
POVERTY

TOWARDS the north of Argyll in western Scotland, across the flat and broken peatland of Rannoch Moor, the mountains of Glencoe rear up suddenly, a natural and forbidding fortress.

For 400 years one small clan occupied the narrow glen enclosed by these mountain battlements. The MacDonalds of Glencoe rarely numbered more than 500 people, and in the harsh climate of the country, life was as much a struggle against the elements as against more mortal enemies. But they survived – independent, unruly, and fiercely proud.

To their wealthier neighbours, they were outlaws. The Campbells of Glenorchy, whose 500 square miles of Highland territory, studded with mighty castles, bordered Glencoe to the south, regarded them as troublesome cattle thieves, an affront to dignity and a threat to peace; they complained about their constant raiding and their scant regard for the law; they branded them 'public enemies to God, the King and his true and faithful subjects'.

Things had once been different. Until the last years of the 15th century, Clan Donald had boasted an empire in Scotland more extensive by far than anything the Campbells now claimed. As Lords of the Isles and Earls of Ross, their lands had stretched from Antrim in Northern Ireland to Dingwall on the north-east mainland of Scotland, a virtual state within a state. To hold it they could call out an army of 10,000 clansmen and mercenaries. When, in 1461, John, Lord of the Isles, proposed a treaty with Edward IV of England, he dealt with him on equal terms. 'Our dearest cousin', Edward called him. At a time when Scotland lacked strong government, the Lords of the Isles challenged the authority of the monarchy itself.

The Glencoe MacDonalds had a share in this heritage. They traced their own roots back to John's great-great-grandfather, Angus Og, Lord of the Isles, who brought 5,000 Highlanders to Bannockburn in 1314 and helped swing the battle in Robert the Bruce's favour, winning for Clan Donald the King's memorable tribute: 'My hope is constant in thee'.

Bruce was generous in his reward and, in the aftermath of victory, ceded the lands of Glencoe, among others, to Angus, who in turn passed the glen itself on to his natural son, Iain Fraoch, John of the Heather. Thereafter the chiefs of Glencoe were known as MacIain, son of John, or Iain Abrach, named after Lochaber, the wild region in which Glencoe lay.

Under the Lordship of the Isles, MacIain succeeded MacIain in undisputed line for generations. But by the end of the 15th century, the ambition of Clan Donald had overreached itself. James IV, aided, significantly, by a Campbell – Colin, first Earl of Argyll – finally challenged the power of the Lordship and found it to be crumbling. In 1493 James sought, and received, its surrender. The decline of MacDonald power had begun.

Among the possessions seized by the Crown was the land of Glencoe. Henceforth its people were to be vassals, first of the Stewarts of Appin, later of the Campbells of Glenorchy and of Argyll. Rarely can landlords have had more troublesome tenants.

The subsequent history of the Glencoe people is documented sketchily, and in a manifestly one-sided manner, from the annals

of those to whom they caused offence. As early as 1500 there is to be found a steady litany of complaints to the Government about their predatory habits and the menace they were said to pose to their neighbours. In that year, for instance, the Earl of Argyll was granted a decree to evict 'John of the Ilis, utherwys Abroch sonne' for cattle raiding – an order which seems to have been ignored. The following year Argyll was further enraged when men from Glencoe launched a daring raid in the heart of Campbell country on the island prison of Innischonnell, where Donald Dubh, heir to the Lordship of the Isles and kidnapped as a child by Argyll himself, was held captive. They managed to break into the prison, remove Donald and escape to the security of their glen.

On that occasion they acted alone, but frequently they would combine with other clans to carry out forays, often over great distances. Their friends were MacDonalds of Keppoch and Glengarry to the north, or MacIains of Ardnamurchan to the west, and with them they would raid, from time to time, through the rich cattle lands of Moray and Lennox, or, if necessary, east as far as Aberdeenshire. Uneasy alliances would sometimes be formed with more powerful clans like the Camerons of Lochiel or the Stewarts of Appin, but these would just as often be broken by sudden and bloody quarrels.

Their deeds of heroism were celebrated in poetry and song long after the Lordship of the Isles had faded into memory. But there were other episodes that reflect on them less honourably. It is plain that they were quite prepared to reach convenient agreements, even with their enemies, if the occasion demanded. In 1563, as Campbell documents relate, 'John Og MacAne Abrycht' (the eighth MacIain of Glencoe) bound himself to serve Colin Campbell of Glenorchy against anyone he might care to challenge – except the Government and the Earls of Argyll. Among other things, this meant helping Glenorchy in his vicious persecution of the MacGregors, a campaign of such violence that it was to become at one point tantamount to genocide. And when, in the latter part of the 16th century, the MacIains were enlisted by the Earl of Argyll to help punish some Ogilvies of Glenisla, they pursued them with such vigour that Lord Ogilvy, in complaining later to the Privy Council in Edinburgh, said that only 'with great difficulty and sore advertisement, he, his wife and his bairns escaped'.

The Privy Council, faced with depositions like this, was empowered to issue instructions for punitive action against an offending clan. It could 'put them to the horn', which made its members outlaws, or, if the matter were truly serious, it might issue 'letters of fire and sword', which entitled any rival chief to take the law into his own hands, to seize land or cattle belonging to the proscribed clan, and to burn its crops or houses. In extreme cases – as against the MacGregors – murder might be sanctioned officially, and the very right of those outlawed to bear their own name forbidden. Sometimes the only evidence the Privy Council required to demonstrate that violence had been done was a shirt soaked in blood.

The Glencoe MacDonalds were never subjected to punishment as extreme as this, but, even so, the nature of the crimes ascribed

Opposite: The River Coe, along whose banks the MacDonalds of Glencoe lived in small settlements

27

to them in the Privy Council records, and their number in proportion to the clan's size, demonstrate at least a determined capacity for insurrection. They were accused of 'reif, houghing, and purpose to murder' [plundering, intending to kill, maiming]; 'hership, spulzie and stouthreif' [driving off cattle, spoiling, brazen thievery]; of 'theft, murder, reif and oppression'. When, in 1603, they joined the MacGregors (the Campbell alliance had not lasted long) in the bloody battle of Glen Fruin against the Colquhouns of Luss, a Glencoe man is reported to have cut the throats of 40 prisoners he was meant to be guarding so that he could return the sooner to the battle. In their feuds with the Stewarts the Glencoe MacDonalds were said to have murdered more of that clan than all the rest of the Stewart's enemies put together.

But these were stories spread mainly by those hostile to them. Glencoe itself was subjected to acts of great brutality. Colin Campbell of Glenlyon – 'mad Colin', a cousin of the Glenorchy Campbells – once caught 36 MacDonalds of Glencoe and their neighbours from Keppoch and hanged them outside his castle as punishment for a cattle raid. The Stewarts of Appin, repaying the deaths of two of their clansmen, were said to have seized the Chief of Glencoe and his brother, executed them, and sent their heads south in a barrel to be exhibited gruesomely to the Privy Council.

The Privy Council records only rarely a MacIain defence to the charges laid against them. In the two cases where a MacIain was actually apprehended and taken to the Tolbooth in Edinburgh to face charges, there is no record of what answer was made to them. But there is no mention of punishment either, which suggests that there might have been a legitimate defence.

The MacIains themselves would doubtless have claimed that most of the crimes laid against their name were committed, either in defence of the clan, or of its dignity. Stealing cattle was a matter of survival or of repaying a debt of honour. The killing of another man might be carried out in self-defence, or to protect the good name of the chief. What no chief could control were the 'broken men' who roamed the Highlands, men who had perhaps been driven from their homes or thrown out by their own clan to fend for themselves in the hills. They owed loyalty to no one chief, and were responsible for more lawlessness than most clan feuds. All too often a troublesome clan like the MacDonalds of Glencoe would find the misdeeds of broken men laid at their door.

On the whole, this was unfair. The MacIains ruled their people with a firm discipline which expected loyalty in return. By and large they received it, and the unity of this tiny clan meant that they held tenure of their glen without a break from the 14th to the 18th century – a remarkable record of durability in violent times.

The symbol of their fierce and continuing independence was the hill country they occupied. Its outpost is the Black Mount, which protects the southern flank of the glen. A narrow entrance leads into a long defile, running first to the west, then bending northwards, protected on both sides by steep escarpments and peaks of forbidding splendour. It is a landscape of towering beauty, but there is no doubting the threat it poses to outsiders when wrapped in bleak weather or the hostility of its inhabitants. Its northern

Right: From the tree-clad
mound of Signal Rock, a
bonfire announced the
approach of an enemy and
rallied the clan

side is protected by the almost continuous cliff-face of the Aonach
Eagach, the Jagged Ridge, 3,000 feet high, stretching from the
narrow mountain track known as the Devil's Staircase at the
eastern end of the glen to the Pap of Glencoe in the north, where it
finally opens out to the waters of Loch Leven. The southern flank
of Glencoe is more broken, but no less fearsome. Two mountains,
the Buachaille Etive Mór and the Buachaille Etive Beag, the
Great and Little Herdsmen of Etive, protect the approaches from
the south-east, then a great mass of interconnected peaks – the
Three Sisters – scarred by fissures and faced by near-vertical cliffs

and scree, punctuate the skyline. In rain the cliff faces run black with water, smooth and treacherous; thick and sudden mists trap the unwary. Narrow gorges, which seem to offer a way through, end only in the massive hulk of Bidean nam Bian, the highest mountain of all. Once in the glen, there is only one way out: nearer its mouth as it twists to the north is Gleann-leac-na-muidhe, a wooded valley leading towards the west, which may, with difficulty, be used as an escape route.

The gentler end of Glencoe lies towards the north and Loch Leven. From the Meeting of the Waters, where three waterfalls crash together in a white cauldron of spray, the River Coe runs first into Loch Achtriochtan, which lies in open meadow-land, then turns north to Achnacon, the Field of the Dogs. Here, in a bend of the river, stands a vast outcrop of ancient limestone known as Signal Rock, surrounded by trees. Tradition has given it several purposes – as an altar for Pictish sacrifices of unspecified nature; as a lookout post; or perhaps as the hill from which a blazing signal might be sent to mark the onset of an attack.

It was between Achtriochtan and Loch Leven that most of Glencoe's people lived, in small settlements at Achtriochtan itself, at Achnacon, Leacantuim, Inverrigan, Carnoch, Laroch, Brecklet, and Invercoe, where their cramped little houses stood around the slightly more solid dwellings of the tacksmen, those who held land by virtue of their close relationship with the chief. Small, squat, damp and dirty, these houses were described by one visitor from the south as 'smoking dunghills'. Yet they were designed with protection from the elements in mind, and closer inspection revealed that they were sensibly made. Built of drystone walls, often as thick as six feet, with a core of sand and earth, they depended for proper shelter on the strength and shape of the timbers used as roofing. These were often hard to come by – already the great forests of the Highlands were disappearing – and if they were not properly cut and fixed, the rain would pour through the roof of turf and thatch, carrying a steady stream of inky-black water down onto the heads of the inhabitants. But if they were well-constructed (and so familiar was the design that they could be built in a day by a willing community), the rain ran down the curved timbers of the roof and through the core of the walls, to drain away into the ground beneath. Held in place by ropes weighted with heavy stones, the peat and rough thatch on top provided solid insulation.

'Nastyness and simplicity' was all one traveller could find to say about their interiors, but they were probably warm enough. Heat was provided by a fire, built on stone flags on the earthen floor of the main room. The smoke rose through an open hole in the roof, or found its way out through the thatch. The fire was kept going all day, and covered with ashes, or 'smoored' to keep it in during the night. It was considered more than just a domestic inconvenience if the fire went out: it meant a year's bad luck for the entire household. A steady heat kept the peat turfs on the roof dry, and the canopy of smoke which hung about the roof-beams gradually coated them with a thick carapace of black tar. Providing heads were kept down (and it is perhaps for this reason that

17th-century furnishings:
an iron candlestick

an ornate caned and
high-backed chair

a gentleman's clothes
press, or wardrobe

Highlanders' chairs were generally short-legged), the air was clear of smoke. Ventilation was through the roof or from what little draught seeped in through the core of the drystone walls.

Within these walls a family lived on terms of considerable intimacy with their animals. Barn, byre, living room and bedroom formed the main areas inside the house, perhaps even in that order of importance; and the only division between each was a thin partition of wood or hanging material. While his cows might sleep on straw, a Highlander lay on heather with the brush upwards; so accustomed was he to this rough springy mattress, it was said, that he would insist on it as bedding even when being entertained in a house where the relative luxury of chaff-filled sacking was in use. His bed was considered a part of his life, and after his death it was ceremoniously burnt.

The animals who shared the Highlander's house and the land around it were his only means of survival. They might be the small, stringy sheep of the Highlands, a few goats, a garron pony, or, if he were well-off, one of the deer-hounds which were much prized in Lochaber country. But what counted most were the sturdy black cattle which were his livelihood, his currency and the best indicator of his wealth. They provided meat, milk, good hide for shield or boot, and once a year were bartered in exchange for meal, iron, fish-hooks, or the luxuries of fine linen and tableware.

Though Glencoe was richer in pasturage than many of its neighbouring valleys, the survival of its cattle through the winter was a yearly struggle. On 1st November, the Festival of Samhain, most of those animals which had not been sold were killed and salted. Of the remainder, barely one in five was expected to survive. The scanty crops of oats, barley and kail, sowed in strips at the foot of the mountains, left minimal fodder; there was no natural hay, and by the time the snows came, the grass had almost disappeared. In winter, reported one traveller, the land was 'gnawed to the quick', and if food were scarce the already feeble cattle might be bled to provide black sausages – a mixture of blood and meal. By the time spring came, the surviving beasts were so weak that they would sometimes have to be carried out to regain their strength.

Life in summer was richer and more pleasant. Traditionally it began on 1st May, the Festival of Beltane, when the Beltane bannock was baked and eaten with custard, or offered as a sacrifice to appease the wild beasts of the glen. Though no wolf had been seen in Glencoe since the early 1600s and the golden eagle rarely threatened the lambs, it was as well to be sure.

With the ending of the feast, the cattle were driven out of the glen to the high ground west of Rannoch Moor where, on the slopes of the Black Mount, the summer shielings were built – simple huts of branches and earth which served as protection while the women made butter and cheese, spun yarn and sang songs, and the men herded the cattle, hunted, or practised the use of arms.

Summer was also the season of another activity for which the clansmen of Glencoe were notorious – cattle raiding. It was partly a matter of economic necessity, partly a way of proving the continuing virility of the clan; the two had become virtually indistinguishable. If the winter had been particularly harsh, then stealing enough to replenish the Glencoe herds might be the only way of surviving the next season. For the young men, taking a *spreich* of cattle from a rival clan was a way of proving their manhood. From the time they were old enough to understand them, they had listened to heroic tales of valour, in many of which the taking of cattle was portrayed as an affair of honour, like the great raid of Cooley, when Ulster, led by the legendary Cuchulain, warred with Connaught over the theft of a vast disputed herd. In their eagerness to emulate these deeds they ranged far and wide beyond Glencoe, seizing a head or two of cattle, or even returning with an entire herd.

Then, if they were pursued, they might drive their booty up a narrow gully in the southern wall of the glen, known as the Coire Gabhail, also as the Hollow of Capture, hidden from sight, where the ground is flat and a stream runs deep underground. Today it is hard to believe that even the sure-footed cattle of the Highlanders could have negotiated this steep and narrow track, but rock-falls have made the pass even more uncertain since then.

From an early age the young men of the clan were trained in the arts of warfare. They were taught first the use of the sword. The heavy two-handed claymore, or Great Sword, used by their ancestors in the 15th century, had been replaced by the more practical basket-hilted sword, which allowed the cut and thrust that was such a deadly part of close-combat work in battle. But to begin with, the youth of Glencoe would practise their strokes with wooden poles, wielding them in bare feet on the moss, under the instruction of their elders.

They learned too the value of the targe, the small round shield fashioned from wood, hide-covered and studded with metal, which could be used on the left forearm as a defence against the enemy's cuts, or as a weapon in itself, capable of inflicting a vicious blow. The dirk, stuck in a belt on the right hip, was for use in emergency at close-quarters, or for despatching a dying foe.

They wore little in the form of protective clothing. By the 17th century the men of fighting age had abandoned the heavy mail shirts once used in battle: everything cumbersome was shed in favour of ease of movement, stealth, and speed.

Summer was also the time for practising the skills of hunting. The traditions surrounding the stalking and killing of the red deer which gathered on the steeps of Bidean nam Bian went back to Fingal – also known as Finn mac Cumhaill – legendary ancestor of the MacDonalds, and to his heroic followers, the Fianna. Stories of the Fianna told of a breed of deer-hounds almost as fearsome as the warriors themselves; these tall rangy animals were still used in the chase – to pursue a wounded beast or to run a stag to ground. The hunter drew on his intimate knowledge of the hill to stalk a suitable stag, then shoot it with flintlock musket or the short yew bow he sometimes carried.

Occasionally a great hunt was organised, with dogs and beaters driving whole herds of deer towards a valley where the hunters would be lying in wait to slaughter them with 'dogs, gunnes, arrows, durkes and daggers', as one English visitor described it.

'The dirk, stuck in a belt, was for use in emergency at close quarters, or for despatching a dying foe'

A fine, large example of the brass brooches worn by women to fasten their plaids

A targe, with animals, interlace and foliage tooled onto its leather covering, and studded with silver nails

An elaborately decorated powder horn

Previous page: The Little
Herdsman of Etive, the
Buachaille Etive Beag,
from the south-east

To the Gaelic poets hunting was akin to battle: 'Taking joy of the
forest and ascending the rough hills, making the blood flow of the
folk of white flank and russet mantle.'

Venison from the hills, salmon and herring from the waters of
Loch Leven, and the rich cheese and butter from the shielings,
meant that the summer seasons in Glencoe could be times of
luxury and relaxation after the privations of winter. For a people
so poor, they knew how to live nobly when circumstances allowed.
More than one traveller remarked on their 'stateliness in the
midst of poverty'.

This cannot be explained by material things alone. There was,
among the clans, a strong respect for religion, education and
culture. One Lowland historian with no liking for the Highlanders
described how they joined 'the pleasures of history and poetry to
those of music, and the love of classical learning to both . . . and
all, even the lowest in station, were sent to school in their youth'.
There is some confirmation of this to be found in the many inscrip-
tions on Highland monuments written in four languages – Gaelic,
English, French and Latin.

A distinction, however, has to be made between the education of
the chief and his relations, and that of the ordinary people. Among
the former it was taken for granted that the young men would go to
schools and universities, either in Scotland – at St Andrew's or
Aberdeen, for instance – or in France. How strictly this applied in
Glencoe is hard to determine, but there is evidence that the chief
and his sons in the 17th century completed their education, by
tradition, in Paris. The Privy Council in Edinburgh laid down that
the ownership of more than 60 head of cattle required a man to
send his children south to be taught to read and write English, but
this was mainly a device to woo the clans away from Gaelic, and in
Glencoe that instruction would have been firmly ignored.

The education of the ordinary people depended largely on the
local parish church and the enthusiasm of its priest. The Mac-
Donalds of Glencoe have been called Roman Catholics because
most of the MacDonald clan in general were Catholic. In the wake
of the Reformation it is difficult to be certain, however: allegiances
often varied from region to region, and in the more remote parts
individual tendencies took hold that obeyed no general rule. One
historian described religion in the Highlands at this time as 'taken
partly from the Druids, partly from papists, and partly from prot-
estants', and superstition certainly went hand in hand with the
Christian faith. But that does not mean that religious instruction
was neglected. As the increasingly hard lines were drawn between
Episcopalians (those who believed in the authority of the bishops)
and Presbyterians (whose church was run by the elders) a remote
parish would often determine its own position by deciding whether
its local minister was effective or not at administering the gospel
and teaching the local children.

The attachment to a good education was as strong in Glencoe as
in other branches of their clan, but those rare visitors from the
south, not understanding Gaelic, found this hard to equate with
what they saw as the grinding poverty of daily life. This was
particularly apparent in the way the ordinary people dressed.

At home in the glen, they wore simply the *léine chrochach*, or long saffron-coloured shirt, beneath a plaid. The young would usually go barefoot, but as they grew older they acquired leather footwear, woollen hose, and the blue bonnets which were the traditional clan headgear.

As MacDonalds, they were entitled to wear a sprig of heather in their bonnets, the only badge that distinguished them from other clans. There were, in the mid-17th century, no clan tartans, only the broad checked fabrics of the plaid, which might vary from region to region, but which had not yet accquired the colours and patterns that would one day distinguish one clan from the next.

The *Feileadh Mór*, or the Big Wrap, as the plaid was known, was a garment for day and night. A vast swathe of cloth, often five feet wide and up to 18 feet long, it was wrapped around the shoulders and arranged in pleats. Belted at the waist, it could be hitched up to give greater freedom of movement, or let down for use as a blanket. The women wore a simpler plaid, the *Arisaid*, checked, with a white background.

This workaday attire gives little idea, however, of the way a chief or his relatives might dress when entertaining guests or travelling to a great occasion. An admiring traveller attending a cattle sale one summer in the Borders described it thus: 'The Highland Gentlemen were mighty civil, dressed in their slashed short waistcoats, a Trousing (which is breeches and Stockings of one piece of striped stuff) with a plaid for a cloak and a blue bonnet. They had a Ponyard, Knife and Fork in one Sheath, hanging at one side of their belt, their Pistol at the other, and their snuff mill before, with a great broad sword by their side. Their attendants were very numerous, all in belted plaids, girt like a woman's petticoats down to their Knees, their Thighs and half of the leg all bare.' More than one traveller noted the bare legs of the Highlander, the 'redshank', as he was called in battle.

There was stateliness in other things too. For the chief and his tacksmen the best claret could be had, imported from France and brought across from the east coast ports by cartload, or north from Glasgow by ship. The consumption of wine in the Highlands was so great at one time that the Privy Council condemned the 'great and extraordinary excesses in drinking wine . . .' and tried to limit consumption to between one and four tuns a year per chief and his immediate relations, a generous allowance amounting to around 500 to 1,000 English gallons a year.

For the poorer folk, beer was more common, and the raw native spirit known as *uisge-beatha* (*aquavita*), later as whisky, was taken by all – though with caution. One Highland writer gave stark warning of its potency: 'At the first taste it affects all the members of the body; two spoonfuls is a sufficient dose, and if any man exceed this, it would presently stop his breath and endanger his life.'

Drink enhanced the entertainment of a long evening, when songs, stories, poetry, dancing and the playing of pipe or mouth music provided a rich repertoire in which all could join. The classical era of Gaelic poetry was over, and with it the highly stylised metres and rigid themes of the great epic poems; although this meant the disappearance of an art-form which could produce a single poem containing no less than 350 adverbs (to celebrate the Battle of Harlaw in 1411), that which followed it was lighter, more accessible, and perhaps more enjoyable. Legends from the days of the Fianna and their battles with the Vikings; stories of witchcraft, spells, and the Second Sight; tales of fairies and goblins, and of An Duine Mór, the Big Man, who was said to walk at night; spinning songs and herding songs, and long nostalgic love poems (many of the best composed by women); and finally poems and songs which looked back to days of the glorious past and spoke of the grief at their passing:

It is no joy without Clan Donald,
It is no strength to be without them,
The best race in the round world,
To them belongs every goodly man . . .

A race the best for service and shelter,
A race the best for valour of hand,
Ill I deem the shortness of her skein
By whom their thread was spun.

For sorrow and for sadness
I have forsaken wisdom and learning;
On their account I have forsaken all things.
It is no joy without Clan Donald

Every chief still had his own bard, ready to celebrate his victories in verse, or bemoan his defeats. And every chief boasted a piper to play the *Ceòl Mór* (the Big Music) or the *Piobaireachd* (*Pibroch*) the intricate classical music of the pipes. It was music for listening to, not for dancing. And the greatest form of it was the lament, composed to mark the death of a great chief or one of his close family. It would be played as they were rowed to their traditional burying ground on the holy island of Eilean Munde, in the middle of Loch Leven, where St Mundus, one of Columba's priests from Iona, had founded a chapel. It was shared ground. Stewarts and Camerons came there too to bury their dead, and there is no record that they ever fought over it.

Both piper and poet celebrated a past which was almost tangible. It was traced back through a long genealogy to the Lords of the Isles and beyond, to Somerled, who founded the Lordship by defeating the Vikings, and to Conn, the semi-legendary Irish God-King, from whom Clan Donald traditionally claimed descent. It was part of the common heritage. Every member of the clan was bound to it, either by ties of blood, or by obligations of loyalty to its chief. From the tacksmen who were related to him, to the dependents or 'native men' who had perhaps always lived on the land he now occupied, to the broken men, or refugees from other clans who had been offered his protection, to the pipers, bards and historians he might employ – all these were part of that unique institution, the Highland clan.

The word clan means literally children or kin, and historians have sometimes waxed romantic over the family nature of the organisation. But there was nothing sentimental about it; the system had been forged by the harsh reality of a violent society, and it carried stern duties on both sides. The loyalty given to a chief was based on the knowledge that he was offering something in return. That might be land, held by the ancient bonds of Friendship, Manrent, or Maintenance, bringing with them dues with names like Steelbow, Tack, Feu, Wadset or Calp, each one with distinct and specific legal obligations. Or it might be simply protection – his ability to provide security against another clan in troubled times, or against a government bent on exacting due revenge for some crime against its authority.

Whatever form it took, the chief of a strong and self-reliant clan offered something which went beyond the purely feudal relationship existing between a Lowland laird and his tenants. If he were a strong chief he would give his people confidence in the unity and continuity of his clan – hence the importance in its make-up of history, genealogy, and pride.

A good chief lived up to the high expectations of his people, remaining close to them but commanding their respect. He knew that if he failed them, they might look to a stronger leader who would take his place. The duties of a chief to his people were widely recognised and were a powerful force for cohesion.

Most important of all was the close connection that every member of the clan could claim with the chief and his family. Whether tied by blood, by oaths of loyalty, or by an allegiance which allowed him to bear the name of his chief, each and every clansman regarded himself as a part of its aristocracy, sharing in 'the great antiquity of his family, and the heroic actions of his ancestors', as one clan historian put it.

This, then, was how they saw themselves, as a people, mid-way through the 17th century. To others – their Campbell neighbours, for instance – there was nothing heroic about them. They were simply hotheads and delinquents, dangerous and unreliable. Their very belief in a glorious past was nothing other than an inability to come to terms with the present.

Overleaf: 'In rain the cliff-faces run black with water, smooth and treacherous . . .' – the southern flank of Glencoe

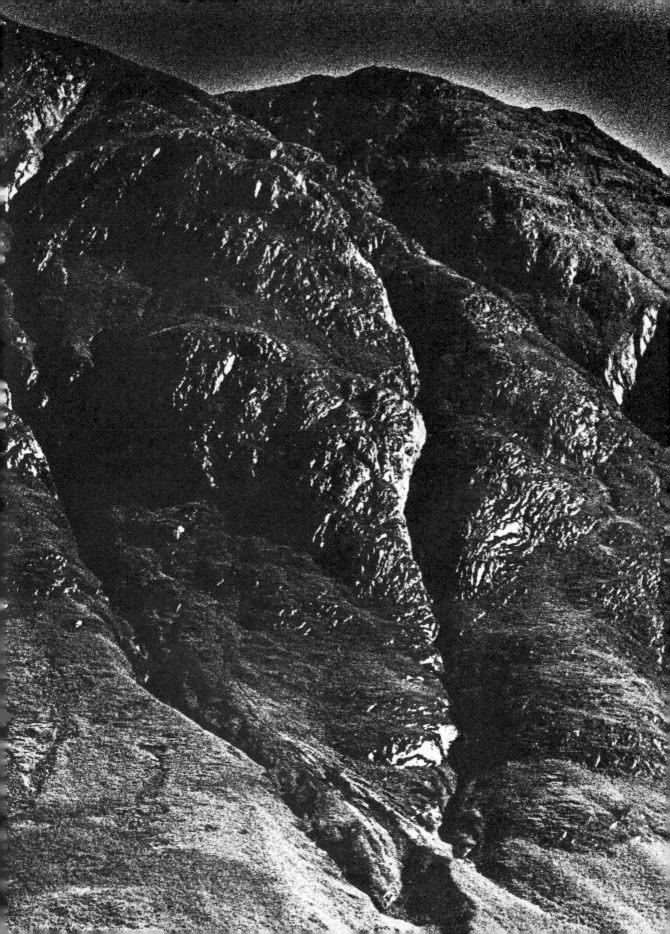

3

'ROOT OUT
THE NAME OF
CAMPBELL'

IN 1640, the year of his death, Sir Colin Campbell, the eighth Laird of Glenorchy and the second most powerful chief in Clan Campbell, undertook an inventory of his possessions. The contents of his four great castles, strung across his estates in central Scotland, bore impressive testimony, not just to the wealth of the Glenorchy Campbells, but to their connections.

As well as the tapestries, silk beds and silver goblets from France, the linen from Flanders, the German paintings and the library rich in French and Italian literature, there were some more personal mementoes: a round shield in enamelled gold, set with diamond, topaz, ruby and sapphire – a gift from King James V; a brooch of gold, set with 29 diamonds and four rubies – a token of esteem from the Queen, Anne of Denmark, to Sir Colin's father; and a precious stone set in silver, worn by the first Laird when, as a Knight of Rhodes, he fought for Rome against the Turks.

Along the corridors of Sir Colin's castle at Balloch, on the eastern corner of Loch Tay, hung 24 portraits of kings and queens, and 34 of his own Campbell ancestors, while at one end of the Great Hall stood the family's genealogy board, which traced their origins back to the 13th-century Knight of Lochow, who fought in the Crusades and returned to found a dynasty which would one day make kings and break them.

More important as a symbol even than these was Sir Colin's foster-child, Archibald Lord Lorne, eldest son of his relative, the Earl of Argyll, whom he had brought up and educated for the past six years at Balloch Castle, supplied with the best tutors, trained in the arts of hunting and the sword, and dressed in coat and breeks of scarlet, silk stockings and a fine French beaver hat.

The importance of Lord Lorne was that he cemented a bond between the two senior Campbell families of Argyll and Glenorchy which was stronger than any formal treaty of friendship. Since Argyll was not only *MacCailein Mór*, Chief of Clan Campbell, but also Justice-General of western Scotland, and the Crown's chief lieutenant, wielding from his stronghold in Inveraray a feudal authority greater than any Highland chief's, his friendship was worth having.

Between them the Argyll and Glenorchy Campbells had ruthlessly enlarged their territory over the past 150 years. But unlike the MacDonalds, who had little use for title deeds or legal documents, they had used the law to establish their rights, buying out tenants whenever possible, extending their borders at the expense of weaker lairds, and at all times playing on their close friendship with the Scottish Crown. The earls of Argyll possessed, in the words of one historian, 'a hereditary capacity for aggrandisement like the Hapsburgs or the Brandenburgs', while even one of their own biographers admitted that the Glenorchy Campbells were driven by 'an insatiable lust for land'. Their neighbours referred to it simply as 'the Greed of the Campbells'.

But within four years of Sir Colin's stately inventory the entire edifice of Campbell power was to be threatened by the might of the Highland clans, and in particular by Clan Donald, bent on revenging the loss of its own empire.

The brilliant Highland campaign of 1644–1646, launched by the

Marquis of Montrose in support of Charles I and against the army in Scotland, was to be a turning-point in relations between Mac-Donalds and Campbells. It gave military shape to a traditional feud which grew more bitter from this stage on: MacDonalds for Montrose, for Royalism, for the Episcopal faith, and ultimately for the Stuart cause; Campbells for Parliament, the Presbyterian Covenanters and the rule of law. It is doubtful, however, if the Glencoe MacDonalds, for their part, saw it in such weighty terms. For them it was first and foremost a war against the Campbells, and the violence with which it was pursued meant that they forfeited for ever the chance of easy relations with their powerful neighbours.

There was no great enthusiasm for King Charles himself. He had, in the early days of his reign, shown little but hostility and contempt for the Highlands, at one point supporting a failed attempt to clear some glens by shipping their inhabitants out to Nova Scotia. But because, by 1644, the Presbyterian Covenanters who opposed him were led by the Earl of Argyll and backed by other Campbell lairds, because the covenanting army looked remarkably like another means of extending the Campbell borders in the name of religion, and because a campaign in support of the King meant a chance of raiding into Campbell country and perhaps regaining lost lands, the royalist cause became, with no great difficulty, the Highland cause as well.

Without Montrose himself and his great general, Alasdair MacColla (better known to history as Sir Alexander MacDonald), the clans could never have united for long, even under this compelling banner. It was Montrose's genius to use them with a sure instinct in battle, and to build them into an army of disciplined élan, in which Irish soldiers, brought by Alasdair from Antrim, combined forces with their Highland counterparts to devastating effect. The result was to be an almost invincible fighting force, in which the Glencoe MacDonalds, though one of its smallest contingents, played a crucial part. Its most dramatic feature was the formidable 'Highland charge', a battle tactic which, for a time, was so effective that even the Government's best-trained troops were unable to withstand it.

The charge had been noted in 1642 at the Battle of Laney in Northern Ireland, when the MacDonnells of Antrim and their Irish allies caught an English army of some 600 men on open ground and cut them to pieces. The tactics the Irish adopted were to be refined later in Scotland, but its essentials remained unchanged for 100 years: the ranks of waiting clansmen would allow the enemy to approach within range, then loose off a volley of musket fire. They would then throw down their guns and charge, with swords and targes, letting out a series of fearsome battle-cries. As they ran they changed formation, from the single musket-line into tight groups, 'like wedges, condensed and firm', as one writer put it. Because the opposing troops had little chance to reload their muskets or fix bayonets once this terrifying array of human fury descended on them, they were often simply cut down where they stood.

Sometimes, to add speed to the charge, the Highlanders would

Opposite: Looking south-
west towards Stob na
Broige and the Lairig
Gartain

throw off their plaids, and then, with their long shirts tied between their legs, would pour down on the enemy half-naked, using targe and sword as double weapons. The opening volley, the battle-cries and the sight of these savage fighters were too much even for hardened veterans. In battle after battle they broke and ran.

In the winter of 1644 Montrose and MacColla, after a series of victories in Aberdeen and Perth, turned west and launched a raid of great brutality into Argyll. It was as unexpected as it was violent, and in the course of it the clansmen ravaged the country and laid waste to the town of Inveraray itself. In the heart of Campbell land a victorious Highland army celebrated a Mass on makeshift altars shielded from the winds by their plaids. The triumphs they hailed had been little more than an orgy of slaughter, much of it cold-blooded revenge, in which 960 Campbells or their allies were killed. Argyll himself escaped from Inveraray by sea, fleeing in ignominy from the advancing army.

Argyll was not the only one to suffer. Glenorchy too was plundered, and Sir Colin Campbell's brother, Robert, who succeeded him, was soon compiling a list more melancholy than the inventory of 1640. Many of his followers had been killed, houses had been deroofed, corn-stacks burnt, cattle driven off. On the south side of Loch Tay only one house was left standing, because it was hidden by trees. The castles held out, but the damage to Glenorchy land was put at £66,000 sterling; the Laird had to buy seed-corn and pay for his tenants' houses to be rebuilt, exposing him to crippling debts.

The MacDonalds of Glencoe had joined Montrose in November 1644, and it was a MacIain relative who advised the army to invade Argyll where, he assured them, there was no lack of cattle to be lifted. The man who led them was Alasdair, the eleventh Chief. He left behind him in Glencoe his son (also called Alasdair) a handsome young boy, aged only 12, who would succeed his father as the twelfth Chief. The events he was now to live through would become part of Glencoe lore, eclipsed only by his own violent end nearly half a century later.

Turning north from Argyll, and guided by a Glencoe man over the passes of the Devil's Staircase, Montrose now headed towards Kilcumin (today Fort Augustus) on Loch Ness. Argyll, furious at the humiliation he had suffered, set off in pursuit and rallied some 3,000 men round the castle of Inverlochy (today Fort William) on Loch Linnhe, 30 miles south-west of Kilcumin.

Montrose, warned that Argyll was preparing for battle, decided to challenge him, despite being outnumbered two to one. In a brilliant flanking movement through the snow-bound mountain passes overlooking the Great Glen, he led his Highlanders across to Inverlochy to take Argyll's army by surprise from the south. With the Glencoe MacDonalds in the vanguard, he launched his attack, after praying for support from the Virgin Mary and two Irish saints, St Patrick and St Brigid.

The Lowlanders in Argyll's army fled almost at once in the face of the Irish and Highland assault. The Campbells held the centre for a time, but finally broke, heading vainly for shelter to the castle itself. They died by their hundreds, cut down by MacDonald

swords. The Covenanters lost almost half their men; Clan Campbell had been humiliated once again; Argyll, watching the battle from his ship in Loch Linnhe, set sail to escape, put to shame in front of his people for the second time.

MacDonald exultation knew no bounds. Iain Lom, Gaelic bard to the Keppoch MacDonalds, a fighter as well as a poet, hammered out a raucous epic to hail the victory:

> *You remember the place called Tawny Field?*
> *It got a fine dose of manure*
> *Not the dung of sheep or goats,*
> *But Campbell blood well congealed.*

For him it was a purely MacDonald victory. Throughout the poem there is no mention of Montrose.

The raid into Argyll and the victory at Inverlochy were astonishing reversals of Campbell fortunes. But they indicated that MacDonalds in the ascendancy could be as vindictive as ever the Campbells had been in the past. In October 1645, the MacDonalds, including men from Glencoe, spent a week ravaging the already impoverished lands of Glenorchy. Then, in December, certain clan leaders met to draw up a plan whose object seems to have been the final elimination of Clan Campbell. Its terms carry with it a grim foretaste of events to come. Sir James Lamont, one of Montrose's allies and a signatory to the agreement the leaders produced, described it as a band drawn up by special envoys of the clans 'bearing in plain terms of combination among us for the ruin of the name of Campbell'. A Campbell historian described it as 'a most cruell horrid and bloody band' for 'rooting out the name of Campbell'.

There is no direct evidence to show that the terms of the band were carried out, but certainly over the next year the Campbells were to become virtual guerillas in their own land, holding on to the great stronghold castles but surrendering land in the face of repeated onslaughts by clansmen under the vengeful Alasdair MacColla. Deprived of the restraining discipline of Montrose, the cause degenerated into clan warfare.

On 4th June 1646, a band of Glencoe men, with others from Keppoch, raided the lands of Sir Robert Campbell at the west end of Loch Tay, rounded up his cattle, and began driving them back towards Rannoch Moor. The Campbell gentry were celebrating a christening at Finlarig Castle when they heard of the raid. Seizing their swords, they set off to waylay the raiders. They caught up with them at the little village of Killin and charged up a ridge 'with thoughtless bravery' to attack them. The MacDonalds turned back on them, and launched a miniature version of their battle charge down the hill. Within minutes the Campbells were overpowered; 30 of them, including four of Glenorchy's nephews, were slaughtered and 21 others wounded. The burn that ran through the corrie where the battle was fought turned red, and was known thereafter as the Bloody Burn.

When the news reached Balloch Castle, a strong body of men armed with guns was despatched in pursuit of the MacDonalds, who were overtaken between Glen Lochay and Glen Lyon. The Campbell soldiers exacted bloody revenge in a long-running battle. Many of the raiders were killed, including Angus Og Mac-Donald, younger son of the Chief of Keppoch. He died in the arms of the Keppoch bard, Iain Lom, who wrote that the death of Angus 'of the pleasant countenance' was sorer to him even than the death of his own father.

MacIains played no further part in Montrose's rebellion, but the way in which Alasdair MacColla's mixed army of Irish and High-landers continued to occupy and ravage Argyll left a deep legacy of bitterness. Terrible events were branded into the consciousness of both sides: the burning to death of Campbell prisoners in a barn at Lagganmore; the massacre of more than 100 members of the Lamont clan at the hands of infuriated Campbell soldiers at Dunoon; the slaughter of 300 clansmen under MacDonald of Sanda at Dunaverty Castle after Sanda had offered to surrender to the besieging army under Cromwell's dour commander, General David Leslie. 'I shall not deny but here was cruelty', wrote Leslie's Adjutant General, 'for to kill men in cold blood, when they have submitted to mercie, hath no generosities at all in it.'

The campaign had opened divisions between Lowlander and Highlander which were to scar the country for 100 years. It had placed the anti-Campbell clans firmly on the side of the King, and, by inference, the Stuart cause. It had emphasised the religious divide between the mainly Catholic clans and the Lowland Presby-terians. And it had aroused among settled Lowlanders a deep fear and hatred of the armed might of the Highlanders.

For Argyll and Glenorchy the next decade was one of painful recuperation. Parliament voted nearly £50,000 to help restore their depleted stocks, and collections were made in churches throughout Scotland to help the poor and aged and to buy seed-corn for farmers.

In Glencoe, however, it was a time of relative security, with the iron grip of the Campbells temporarily eased. In 1650, Alasdair MacDonald became the twelfth MacIain, succeeding his father as chief of the Clan Iain Abrach in the old Gaelic ceremony in which, by tradition, he stood on top of a pyramid of stones surrounded by his warriors. He was in his mid-twenties, a red-headed giant of a man, said to have been all of six feet seven inches tall. Whether he had yet cultivated the great curling mustachios for which he was to be famous is unknown, but he was undoubtedly a formidable figure, broadly built, dark-eyed, and with a fierce beak of a nose.

He lived in the midst of his clan, dividing his time between two houses. One, the largest in Glencoe, was at Carnoch, somewhere towards the mouth of the glen, though its exact location is dis-puted. It was probably two storeys high, lime-washed and roofed with the local slate, furnished inside with hangings, lace, glass and silver – objects unfamiliar to most of his clansmen.

Some of these decorations he may have brought with him from France, where he had spent some time in his youth, learning the French language and acquiring a taste for the trappings of civilis-ation. In France a Highland chief was treated by the nobility not just as an equal but as the honoured representative of an ancient ally. The contrast between the fine houses of Paris in which he was entertained and the poor glens from which he came was enormous, but on his return he would bring mementoes of his visit as well as an appreciation for the finer things of life. More than one traveller of the time was moved to comment that you could pass a more elegant evening in the company of a remote Highland laird than you could in some of the noble houses of England.

MacIain's summer house was a mile or two off the glen to the west of Achnacon, in the broad mossy valley of Gleann-leac-na-muidhe. Its ruins are still marked there today – more, perhaps, from optimism than certainty. A simpler dwelling than the one at Carnoch, it was still sturdier than most Glencoe cottages.

Alasdair was to marry a MacDonald of Keppoch, whose people were the MacIains' closest allies; he had two sons and a daughter. John, the eldest, would succeed him, and Alasdair Og, the younger son, would carry on, at a later stage of the Highland rebellion, the tiny clan's tradition of warlike independence.

In 1655 the MacDonalds of Glencoe again raided Glenorchy territory: with the Keppoch MacDonalds they swept down Glen Lyon, burning, looting, and driving off cattle. This time they were delayed on their return by a young Campbell dairy-maid, who was said, by legend, to have broken the legs of one of the calves the MacDonalds had seized. The lame calf slowed their progress back towards Rannoch Moor, and they were overtaken. In another brutal encounter many dead and wounded were left behind before the Glencoe men managed to reach safety.

But MacIain's reputation remained high among his friends. He was described as 'strong, active, and of the biggest size, much loved by his neighbours, blameless in his conduct . . .' He had 'integrity, honour, good nature and courage'. To others, however, in particular his neighbours to the south, he was an untrustworthy renegade. To Archibald, ninth Earl of Argyll, he was a dangerous trouble-maker, an ally of his enemies (in particular the Macleans, with whom he was conducting a long war), and possibly a murderer.

The violent death of one of MacIain's own clansmen was reported to the Privy Council, and, in 1674, in his capacity as Justice-General of Argyll and the Isles, Argyll managed to have MacIain seized and committed to prison in the Tolbooth at Inveraray. The Privy Council report on MacIain's crime is unspecific:

'He and John MacDonald of Achtriochtan, with divers of their people, have committed several murders and depredations whereby the country in these parts is like to be casten loose and exposed to the rapine and violence of these people.'

For offences such as these MacIain would undoubtedly have faced the hangman. Merely to be held prisoner in the capital of Campbell territory was an appalling disgrace, the first recorded time that a Glencoe chief had been held captive by Campbells. But within a few months MacIain was free. There is no means of telling how he escaped from his prison in Inveraray, but escape he undoubtedly did. The Privy Council was moved to write angrily to Sir James MacDonald of Sleat, who was held responsible for his behaviour at the time, urging him to help apprehend MacIain, 'and that your care and diligence in

this will be answerable to the obligation that lies on you . . .'

Sir James was unable, or unwilling, to oblige. And soon afterwards the authority of Argyll himself was undermined. The balance of power in the Highlands was shifting. Charles II had sent his brother, James, Duke of York, to Scotland, with the specific object of pacifying the Highlands, and James had decided that the power of Argyll should be reduced. Argyll was on the wrong side of the religious dispute between Presbyterians and Episcopalians, and though he attempted to pursue a moderate line, the Test Act of 1681 – which required him not only to acknowledge royal supremacy, but never to alter the *status quo* in Church and State – set him an impossible choice. He attempted to swear a version of it, but then, courageously, refused. He was tried for treason and condemned to death, but managed to escape from Edinburgh Castle disguised as a page-boy.

When James succeeded his brother Charles II as king in 1685, Argyll decided to support Charles's bastard son, Monmouth, in his claim to the throne. He returned to Scotland from exile in Holland to raise a rebellion on Monmouth's behalf. It was a doomed venture. Argyll was captured, taken to Edinburgh, and executed on the 'Maiden', the Scottish equivalent of the guillotine, climbing the steps to his death with a quiet courage which impressed even his enemies.

In the aftermath of Argyll's execution, a clan army, which had been raised by the Privy Council to oppose Argyll's rebellion, was led by the Marquis of Atholl into Argyll country. The Atholl raid, as it was known, can only be described as official pillage. MacIain and his kinsmen took part in it, and made good use of this venture into some of the richest lands in Campbell hands. They swept through the estates of Kilbride, Carrick, Kenmore, Ardkinglas and Rosneath. They looted or burnt whatever they could lay their hands on, irrespective of whether or not the owners had supported Argyll's rebellion. As well as livestock, they took several valuable possessions. John MacDonald, MacIain's eldest son, took from one Campbell of Ardentinny, 'pewter plates, whole glass windows, a great house bible, Josephus his works, Turk's Historie, Polybius, the Countess of Pembroke's Arcadia, with several other great volumes, together with several small grammar authors', as Ardentinny later complained to the Privy Council.

MacIain himself was more prosaic. From Rosneath he took cows, horses, sheep, goats and household goods to the tune of nearly £1,000 Scots (about £83 sterling). Crops, houses, boats and barns were burnt.

Once again Argyll country had been pillaged at the hands of MacDonalds – only this time with the connivance, if not the active encouragement, of the Government. It is perhaps small wonder that efforts to pacify the Highlands deteriorated. By 1688 they had lapsed into a state where theft and banditry were rife, and the Government was seemingly incapable of controlling what a Royal Commission called 'the incursions, depredations and the barbarous cruelty of thieves, sorners and broken men' who ravaged the southern and central Highlands.

When, in that year, the MacDonalds of Keppoch met their age-old enemies, the Mackintoshes, at Mulroy, in what is generally held to be the last clan battle, the MacDonalds won the day in spite of the fact that the Government gave its support to the Mackintosh faction.

On the surface it seemed as if the MacDonalds of Glencoe were as secure in their valley stronghold as they had ever been: Argyll's heir, Lord Lorne, unable to persuade James II to restore his land and titles, had fled the country to join William of Orange in Holland; and in Glenorchy the eleventh Laird was concentrating too hard on the old Campbell preoccupation of building up and extending the family estates to concern himself with the unruly valley to the north.

But events were soon to change dramatically. In the next few years the House of Argyll was to be restored to heights more commanding than any it had achieved before. And the man who was now Campbell of Glenorchy would sow the seeds of a plan to ruin Glencoe for ever.

Overleaf: Loch Leven looking east towards Glencoe

53

4

'THE BARBARIAN PRIDE OF A HIGHLAND CHIEF'

THE eleventh Laird of Glenorchy was a Campbell to his finger-tips. As a young man impatient for wealth, he had, to the great resentment of his father, taken over the running of the family's estates, bankrupt in the wake of Montrose's war, and set about building them up again. In a series of ruthless financial deals, he not only restored Glenorchy lands to their former glory but expanded their boundaries still further. The family motto was brief and to the point: 'Conques, or keip thingis conquest'.

By the time he was 50 in 1685, he had been raised to the Scottish peerage as Earl of Breadalbane, and was a power to be reckoned with in the council chambers of the land. Twice married, he had seen to it that both matches brought handsome dowries and new titles. He had bought the earldom of Caithness by paying the debts of the penniless Earl and then, when he died, marrying his widow; and he had reinforced his claim by marching a clan army north and routing the men of Caithness in pitched battle. King Charles II had confirmed him in his new title until he learned that the claim was based 'upon gross and false representations', at which point Glenorchy was obliged to restore the earldom to its proper owner. But he still managed to compile a handsome tally of honours: he was officially Earl of Brea D'Albane and Holland, Viscount of Tay and Paintland, Lord Glenorchie, Benderaloch, Ormelie and Wick in the Peerage of Scotland. He was known to his clansmen as 'Grey John', but it is as Breadalbane that history remembers him.

Breadalbane had not, in the course of his acquisitions, won many friends. John Macky, a contemporary observer of the political scene, described him as 'cunning as a fox, wise as a serpent, slippery as an eel. No government can trust him but where his private interest is in view.' General Hugh Mackay, commander of the Government's forces in Scotland, called him 'the cunningest temporiser in Britain'. And the historian Macaulay put his finger on the true contradiction in his character when he wrote: 'In his castle among the hills he had learned the barbarian pride and ferocity of a Highland Chief. In the Council Chamber at Edinburgh he had contracted the deep taint of treachery and corruption.'

He was an impressive-looking man, square-jawed, thin-lipped, cold-eyed, with a hooked nose and imperious bearing; he commanded respect and loyalty from his tenants and the Campbell gentry who ran his estates. He had been brought up on the history of Glenorchy, since his tutor had helped Sir Colin Campbell compile his inventory of possessions in 1640 and had written an account of the family. He was determined that the House of Glenorchy should never again be subjected to the ravages which had so nearly destroyed it, and that it should command at least as great an influence in Scotland as the House of Argyll.

This ambition was to involve him in some delicate political balancing acts. He had shown apparent devotion to the Stuart cause by supporting both Charles II and his brother James II, and had avoided the crisis of conscience which had been so unhelpful to his cousin the Earl of Argyll.

In 1688 these loyalties were put severely to the test by the accession to the throne of William of Orange. In November of that year William landed at Torbay in Devon and advanced on London, whence James II, after long hesitation, finally fled, disguised as a Thames boatman, and went into exile in France.

Breadalbane's reaction was cautious. He allowed himself to be linked to a powerful cabal of Scottish nobles who offered support to William: they included Viscount Tarbat, formerly James II's chief minister in Scotland, the Marquis of Atholl, and Sir John Dalrymple, a future Secretary of State. But Breadalbane was careful at the same time to keep his new allegiance as quiet as he could, at least in the Highlands, where he could profess to be still sympathetic to the Jacobite cause.

Then, in May 1689, the clans rose on behalf of the exiled King James, pledged to restore him to the throne of Scotland and to throw out the 'usurper' William. Once again they had a leader capable of inspiring them to greatness. John Graham of Claverhouse, Viscount Dundee – 'Bonnie Dundee', as history recalls him – knew how to handle the chiefs, and commanded enormous loyalty from them. 'So great was the confidence they reposed in his conduct', said the biographer of one of them, Sir Ewen Cameron of Lochiel, 'that they resigned themselves intirely to his pleasure, without searching into his designes.'

The call went out to the clans to rally on the field of Dalcomera in the Great Glen. Camerons, MacDonalds, Macleans of Duart, Stewarts of Appin, MacNeills, MacLeods and many others gathered in front of Dundee, a superbly romantic figure, mounted on his charger, dressed in a scarlet cloak, with green leaves in his bonnet.

Leading 120 of his warriors from Glencoe was MacIain, by now in his sixties and one of the oldest chiefs there, his hair white, his mustachios curled upwards, wearing a buff coat and carrying a brass blunderbuss, both famous trophies of war. He was flanked by his two sons, John and Alasdair, his piper, and a group of young men chosen as his bodyguard. There is a contemporary ode to MacIain at Dalcomera written by James Philip of Almerieclose, Dundee's standard-bearer, a gentleman whose emotions were clearly stirred by the colours of the plaids and the strident music of the war pipes:

Nixt with a dareing look and warlike stride
Glencoe advanced: His rattleing armour shone
With dreadful glare: His large, broad, brawny back
A thick bull's hide impenetrably hard,
Instead of Cloath's invest, and though allong
Twice fifty of gigantick limbs and size
The warrior led, feirce, hardy, wild and strong,
Yet his vast bulk did like a turret rise
By head and shoulders o'er the surly crew.
Round, in his left, his mighty shield he twirled,
And in his right, his broad-sword brandished high,
Which flashed like lightning with affrighting gleams.
His visage boisterous, horribly was graced
With stiff mustachios like two bending horns,
And turbid firey eyes, as meteors red,
Which fury and revenge did threaten round.

There was, of course, no sign of Breadalbane among these mighty chiefs, though Dundee still appears to have considered him an ally. A month after Dalcomera, Dundee wrote to a friend: 'I had almost forgot to tell you of my Lord Breadalbane who, I suppose, will now come to the fields'. Somehow he never did.

On 17th July 1689, Dundee's 2,500 Highlanders fought their first and finest battle at Killiecrankie. The Government's army of some 3,000 foot-soldiers, backed by cavalry and dragoons, was commanded by the capable and experienced Major General Hugh Mackay, a Highlander himself from Scourie in Sutherland, who had seen service in the Dutch wars. Mackay had set out to march from Perth north through Dunkeld to recapture the Marquis of Atholl's castle of Blair, which commanded the main route to Inverness. He passed through the narrow gorge of Killiecrankie, and then rested his army in the more open valley beyond it.

Suddenly Dundee's Highlanders appeared on the slopes overlooking them. Mackay ordered his soldiers into a long line where they hurriedly prepared for battle. Dundee approached to just beyond musket shot, then halted. Mackay ordered his field pieces to open fire, but still the Highlanders waited, the clans drawn up in their traditional formations, with Clan Donald on the left flank. Then, half an hour before sunset, to a terrific shout of encouragement from Cameron of Lochiel, they charged, halted, opened fire with their muskets, then threw them aside and ran on. Plaids as well as guns were discarded, as the clansmen poured down the hills, yelling their battle-cries. The waiting infantry

Above: The strange and sinister landscape of Rannoch Moor

fired, and the withering shots brought down at least 600 men. But it failed to stop the charge. As the redcoats struggled to screw bayonets into the muzzles of their muskets, the Highlanders were on them, broadswords whirling and cutting, targes clouting weapons aside, dirks plunging.

Mackay's troops turned to run. Under a lesser general it would have been a rout, but Mackay managed to pull back in good order as darkness began to fall. Even as he did so, however, the news was beginning to spread among the victorious Highlanders that Dundee himself was dead. He had been shot and mortally wounded as he led a small troop of Highland cavalry in the centre of the battle, and he was carried from the field to be buried amid scenes of great mourning in the churchyard at Blair.

Dundee's death was a blow which crippled the campaign. There was no leader of comparable qualities to take his place. Iain Lom, the Keppoch bard, spoke of the 'great load of sorrow' the clans would now have to bear, and Lochiel recalled that 'he seemed formed by heaven for great undertakings'. Among the government troops, however, 'Bluidy Clavers', as he was known, was supposed to have made a pact with the Devil; people muttered that the bullet which killed him must have been made of silver.

His death signalled the rapid end of the rising. The Glencoe men, along with others, agreed to serve on under Dundee's successor, Colonel Cannon, but their next encounter, at the battle of Dunkeld, was a disaster: the Highland charge failed to make its expected impact on a small but seasoned body of troops, the Presbyterian Cameronians, who held the town, and, in the street-fighting that followed, the remnants of Dundee's clan army broke and ran, leaving 300 dead behind them among the smoking ruins.

MacIain remained pledged to the Jacobite cause. He had signed a bond, with other chiefs, announcing himself ready to serve James, and to bring 50 men to the field if the call went out again. The agreement meant that he was now documented, in the eyes of the Government, as a rebel and an outlaw. It was a status to which he was well accustomed.

From the ruins of Dunkeld he took his people home. Along with his old allies, the Keppoch MacDonalds, he set out on a well-tried route along the shores of Loch Tay. The homeward raid they now carried out, on Breadalbane's land and that of his kinsmen, was unopposed. Breadalbane had finally signalled his intention of throwing in his lot with General Mackay, and had offered him one of his castles as a garrison; but he had not posted soldiers. The MacDonalds took the garrisoning as an act of war, and set about ravaging the land from Loch Tay to Rannoch Moor. They attacked and destroyed what they could of Breadalbane's castle at Achallader, burnt the cottages around it, and drove off the cattle.

The man who suffered worst at their hands, however, was not Breadalbane himself but his cousin, Robert Campbell of Glenlyon, who was already bankrupt. Glenlyon had secured from Colonel Cannon a letter of protection, which, in view of his financial circumstances, Cannon had made out in the name of Campbell's wife. It was of no avail. The MacDonalds of Keppoch and Glencoe swept through Glenlyon, taking the Laird completely off his guard. The women and cattle had just come home from the shielings, and the men were still harvesting. Relying on Cannon's protection, they had taken no precautions, and no attempt was made to prevent the ravaging of their land. What little Glenlyon had left was taken. He lost 36 horses, 240 cows, 993 sheep, 133 goats and all his household goods. Relating the disaster afterwards, his followers claimed that the MacDonald raiders had even turned a baby out of its cradle so they could steal the blanket the child was wrapped in.

When the final reckoning was made, Glenlyon calculated that his losses totalled nearly £8,000 Scots (about £670 sterling). For him it was the last blow. The letter of protection he had been given was as little use to him as letters of a similar kind were to be in Glencoe some three years later. At the age of nearly 60, he would be forced to take up a military career to earn his living – a role which was to have terrible consequences for Glencoe.

MacIain returned home in the autumn of 1689 with enough and more to see his people through a hard winter. Together with the Keppoch MacDonalds they were now, more than ever, branded as public enemies. They were named in Privy Council proclamations as murderers, traitors and rebels.

As one Campbell historian saw it: 'At the era of the Revolution [of William III] Coll of Keppoch and MacIain of Glencoe had vindicated the right of waging private war and of living by the systematic plunder of the sword as freely as any ancestors of the Isles had done hundreds of years before . . .'

It was not a right that would be tolerated for very much longer.

Overleaf: The entrance to the Hollow of Capture, where the Glencoe men often concealed the cattle they had stolen

5

FAIR WORDS
AND
FALSE TREATIES

'We are willing to convince all our subjects of our affection and tenderness towards them by the evidence of an equal and moderate government . . . but if any be so incorrigible or so foolish as to be imposed upon by vain suggestions to make their native country the stage of war and desolation, it will be your care [the Privy Council's] to discover their designs and secure such persons that they be not in a capacity to ruin themselves and others.'

KING William's attitude towards his Highland subjects was mainly one of irritation. He resented the trouble they caused him at a time when he was preoccupied with his wars on the Continent. He grudged every penny spent keeping the peace among them, instead of building up his army in Flanders. And he could see no good reason why those savages of the north, whom he knew to be excellent soldiers, should not be fighting in his regiments, rather than stirring up trouble against him. But he was not, at least to begin with, vindictive. At his investiture in 1689, he had sworn not to be a persecutor, and, at the time, he probably meant it. He listened to Queen Mary, better disposed to the clans than he, and, in his frequent absences abroad, left her to deal, as often as possible, with Highland matters.

In the aftermath of Killiecrankie, however, William was urged by General Mackay, his commander in Scotland, to take sterner action against the rebels. The Highlands should be garrisoned with a string of forts, thought Mackay, and force met with force. William's first reaction was to delay. Forts cost money, and others were urging gentler means. The Earl of Breadalbane, for instance, proposed a plan to bribe the chiefs into laying down their arms. £5000 or £6000 sterling, he thought, might do the trick, if he could 'meet, treat and correspond with any of the Highlanders in order to reduce them to submission and obedience'.

In April 1690, that plan was overtaken by events. Two of King James's officers, Thomas Buchan and Alexander Cannon, raised the Stuart standard and called out the clans. This time fewer than 1500 men turned out (they included a party from Glencoe under MacIain's fiery son Alasdair Og), and they were dismally routed at the battle of Cromdale, when a small force of dragoons under Sir Thomas Livingstone caught them, unprepared, in a misty dawn and took 400 prisoners.

The rising coincided with rebellion in Ireland, which William himself quelled at the Battle of the Boyne, and he agreed that the time had come for Mackay to construct his forts. From this followed two decisions which would intimately affect the events of the next two years. One was the building of the garrison at Inverlochy – to be renamed Fort William. The other was the appointment, as its governor, of Colonel John Hill.

Both the building and the man had been there before. Under Cromwell, when the Highlands had known a brief period of calm, a great fort of timber and ramparts, held by ten companies of foot, had commanded the entrance to the Great Glen. Major John Hill, as he then was, had exercised full authority over the surrounding area. He had established good relations with the clans, particularly with Cameron of Lochiel, who had promised allegiance and

had helped ensure as much peace as was compatible with traditional clan attitudes. 'A man may ride all over Scotland with a switch in his hand and £100 in his pocket,' reported Cromwell's commander, General Monck, 'which he could not have done these five hundred years'.

With the restoration of Charles II, all that Hill had achieved was swept aside. Lochiel marched into the fort, accepted the Governor's keys and burnt the garrison of Inverlochy to the ground. With its destruction, the Government's writ in Lochaber ceased to run.

By 1690 Colonel Hill, now in his sixties, had begun to think fondly of that period, and was anxious to return to the Highlands. He had spent the intervening years in Dublin, as an aide to the Lord Lieutenant of Ireland, the Earl of Essex, but he longed for proper military service and believed that he knew how to deal with the Highlanders. Through his close friendship with the Forbes family of Culloden, and others who recalled his earlier service, he quietly began lobbying for a new appointment. When, in July 1690, work began on reconstructing the garrison at Inverlochy, Hill was considered a natural choice as governor.

The fort was dug into flat ground protected on three sides by water, and on the fourth by marshland. It was palisaded and protected by a rampart of stone, earth and timber 20 feet high. Twelve naval guns, borrowed from two of Mackay's frigates, which had been sent up to patrol the coast, poked out of loopholes. Inside, there was accommodation and protection for six officers and 96 private soldiers, though it was frequently stretched to cater for far more.

Hill was given his own regiment, drawn from various disbanded companies, and he was joined by Captain John Forbes of Culloden, brother of the third Laird, with whom he was on affectionate terms. But things were not the same as they had been in Monck's time. For one thing, Hill was to find his time as governor dogged by a persistent shortage of money and equipment. His letters to Edinburgh show mounting frustration at the penny-pinching forced upon him – just to keep his soldiers in uniform. The lack of money and the wretched conditions at the garrison, in the first months of its existence, meant that the soldiers at Fort William were in an almost permanent state of semi-mutiny. Hill himself was far from well: in the winter of 1690 he suffered a feverish attack which almost cost him his life, and he was never thereafter in good health.

The clans, for their part, showed little readiness to be friendly. Supply trains were attacked and robbed by bands of marauding clansmen, making the sea route up Loch Linnhe the only safe way of bringing provisions. No chief was yet prepared to offer his allegiance to King William, and even Cameron of Lochiel kept his distance. At his castle, 20 miles away, Alasdair MacDonald of Glengarry was actually entertaining one of the exiled King James's officers, Sir George Barclay; Colonel Cannon was still said to be in the Highlands.

Yet, there was no outright hostility. Not even the rumours from England that year of a French invasion had sparked off any major trouble. Some of the lesser lairds and tacksmen had even presented

themselves at the fort to ask for letters of protection, which Hill had been glad to give. They had included a cousin of MacIain's, John MacDonald of Achtriochtan, who had been given Hill's undertaking that he would be safe from any government action, provided he guaranteed to keep the peace. Agreements like this had no binding force on the chiefs themselves, but they were at least a sign of progress which Hill could report to his superiors.

Hill's main confidant in Edinburgh was George Mackenzie, Viscount Tarbat, who still carried considerable influence and was close to the Secretary of State, the Earl of Melville. Hill's view, reinforced by an unexpected visit to the fort from Coll, chief of the Keppoch MacDonalds, was that if the Government could win over some of the greater chiefs, then the others might well be prepared to follow. The way to do that might be to offer them money.

'If the King would cast a little largesse upon Lochiel (who rules all the rest), Glengarry and MacLean who are low in the world, and the rest, must do as they do, and the value of five or six thousand pounds would do the work and make them the King's true servants.'

This was much the same kind of sum Breadalbane had proposed, but Hill was deeply suspicious of the motives of a man of Breadalbane's reputation. He began to wonder what the noble earl was plotting, and was convinced that nothing good would come of his involvement.

It was Tarbat in Edinburgh who put his finger on the one proposal that stood a real chance of wooing the clans over to William. If money could be spent, he thought, not just on bribery but on buying out the feudal rights of those powerful nobles who stood between the clans and the King, then a major source of friction would be removed. Thus a MacDonald chief, for instance, would owe his allegiance direct to the Crown rather than to the Earl of Argyll, who was his feudal superior. Tarbat's advice to the King therefore was:

'One thing all the clans desire, which is as much to your advantage as theirs, which is that all these superiorities be bought from the Highland lords so that [the chiefs] may hold their estates immediately of you; and having them as immediate vassals, keeping a little garrison in Lochaber, and a man of ability, being no Highlander, to be your lieutenant-governor there, you will indeed be master of the Highlands as ever King of Scotland was.'

There is no doubt that, if this idea had been pursued, the events of the following year, indeed the whole subsequent history of the Highlands, might have been different. But it had one severe drawback. It would, at a stroke, remove the hereditary power of those, such as Argyll and Breadalbane, whose feudal role was fundamental to the wealth and influence they enjoyed. Tarbat's plan, therefore, though approved of in principle, won no support from those who might have made it work.

Instead, Breadalbane began in the spring of 1691 to move into the forefront of events. His own plan, submitted directly to the King, was entitled 'Proposals Concerning the Highlanders', and it contained one central idea which he knew would appeal to William.

If the clans could be bought, he argued, then their fighting men might be used for service in the King's army rather than for their endless clan feuds. The price, however, had risen somewhat. Instead of the modest £5000 or £6000 he had originally suggested, the sum of £20,000 was what he now had in mind.

In May 1691 Breadalbane travelled to London where, since William was in Flanders, he spoke to Queen Mary and her ministers. His plan was considered and submitted to Parliament. They baulked at the price, but agreed finally on £12,000. The money was lodged in London in Breadalbane's name while he travelled north to persuade the chiefs to accept it.

The meeting took place on 30th June at Breadalbane's castle at Achallader, the building attacked two years before by the MacDonalds of Keppoch and Glencoe on their way back from Killiecrankie; its timbers still lay charred from the experience. The fact that the clan chiefs agreed to come at all was surprising. Breadalbane was widely distrusted, not just as a Campbell, but as a man believed to be playing a double game. The men he met at Achallader were aware that he had once offered support to Dundee, but had then thrown in his lot with William. He was, they knew, 'Willie's man in Edinburgh and Jamie's in the Highlands'.

In spite of their suspicions, however, the chiefs clearly thought there was merit in seeing whether a realistic treaty might be reached. Their loyalty was still to James, but it was not entirely blind, and a workable peace was something to be welcomed. Besides, if it were true that Breadalbane was going to distribute English gold, then that was certainly nothing to be spurned. The men who came to Achallader were MacDonalds of Glengarry, Keppoch and Glencoe, Stewarts of Appin, Camerons of Lochiel, Macleans of Duart and other chiefs who had sworn oaths to King James. They came with their bodyguards and their pipers, and they were accompanied by General Thomas Buchan and Sir George Barclay, James's officers in Scotland.

Accounts of what took place at Achallader during the three weeks of bargaining that followed vary wildly: with so many conflicting interests involved that was inevitable. Breadalbane's own version is the smoothest – but the least reliable. According to him an amicable discussion took place, and the chiefs agreed to a resolution under which they would keep the peace until October. During that time Breadalbane undertook to obtain and distribute the money he had promised them. The officers representing King James would be given passes enabling them to go overseas. 'They left in good hopes to receive the money', continued Breadalbane's account, 'and an indemnity when they disbanded and dismissed all their men, and I went straight to London, where I gave the Queen and her ministers an account of what passed. From thence I went to the King in Flanders and represented the whole affair in its true and full state wherewith his Majesty was well pleased.'

His Majesty might have been less pleased if he had been given some of the other versions.

MacIain of Glencoe, for instance, had quarrelled openly with Breadalbane, who had not attempted smooth words with a man who had so recently pillaged his land. MacIain was informed that

any money due to him would be kept back to pay for the cattle stolen by him and his men on their way back from Killliecrankie. He responded furiously by pointing out that a treaty which promised remission for killing government soldiers at Killiecrankie, but refused it for the theft of a few cows, was not worth signing. Gathering his men, he informed them brusquely that neither the treaty nor the man proposing it were honourable enough to detain them, and then left for Glencoe. 'There's bad blood between our family and his,' he told his sons. 'I fear mischief from no man so much as the Earl of Breadalbane.'

Other chiefs at Achallader were treated more respectfully. Breadalbane sought them out one by one, assuring them of their share of the money, promising favourable treatment by the Government if they would sign his treaty. Its terms were strictly limited: it merely required the chiefs and those under arms for King James in Scotland to suspend hostilities for the next three months – until 1st October. In return the Government would call off all military action against them.

One of the first to agree, surprisingly, was Coll MacDonald of Keppoch. Others followed suit, though Alasdair MacDonald of Glengarry, whose house guests were Buchan and Barclay and who was a staunch Jacobite, was not pleased to discover that the £1,500 he thought he had been promised was only to be £1,000. He returned to his formidable castle and set about refortifying it.

The influential Cameron of Lochiel also signed, though he suspected that Breadalbane could not be fully trusted to part with all the money. His agreement was important, since although Lochiel was related to Breadalbane through his mother (a Glenorchy Campbell), he was a formidable old man and as independent as any of the chiefs. He had sworn not to submit, 'let the terms be never so inviting, until I have my master's permission to do it'.

And there, possibly, lay the secret reason for Breadalbane's success. What he failed to report to William was that in the course of negotiations he had conceded an important principle: that the chiefs were still bound to another king. They had signed oaths of loyalty to James at Dalcomera and later at Blair Castle, and until they were released from them it was inconceivable that they could swear allegiance to William. Breadalbane agreed that, until their promises to James were revoked, no long-term agreement would be asked of them. They in their turn would send emissaries to Paris asking James to give them his release.

Breadalbane almost certainly went further. A rumour began to circulate that he had offered the Highlanders, along with the official Treaty of Achallader, a series of private undertakings. Within a few weeks of the signing, the extent of these so-called Private Articles was being talked of in Edinburgh. It was said that Breadalbane had virtually conceded the Jacobite case by agreeing that the chiefs would be released from their limited oath to William if James II decided to launch an invasion; that if James did not approve the treaty it would be automatically void; and finally, that Breadalbane had agreed to join the rebels himself and back a Jacobite rising with a thousand men if William were to break the terms of the treaty.

Opposite: Beinn Fhada, one of the Three Sisters of Glencoe

Overleaf: Glencoe's only loch, Achtriochtan, seen from the west

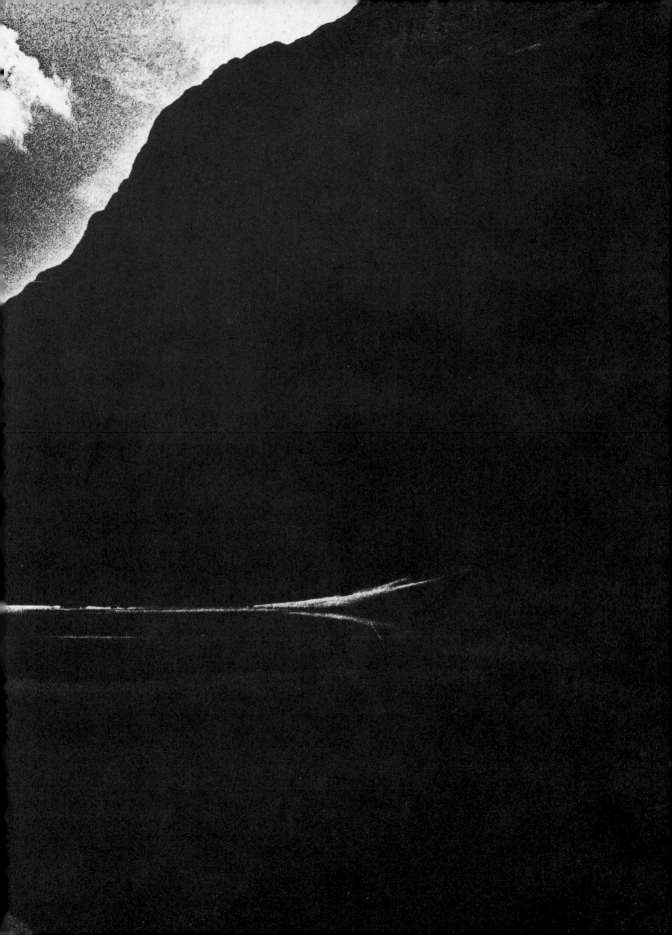

The rumoured existence of the Private Articles was quickly used as a weapon by Breadalbane's enemies. Colonel Hill at Fort William was one of the first to hear the story, possibly from Glengarry, and he passed it on to his political masters in Edinburgh. Eventually it reached the ears of William himself and his joint Secretary of State for Scotland, the Master of Stair.

Breadalbane immediately denied the charge. 'Malicious coffee-house stories', he called it, and hurried back to Scotland to meet the chiefs again, demanding to know whether they intended to renege on the agreement they had made.

The Master of Stair wrote to him soothingly: 'No one believes your Lordship capable of doing either a thing so base, or that you could believe there could be any secret treaties, where so many ill eyes upon your proceedings; but . . .', he added ambiguously, 'the truth will always stand fast.'

William himself was brisker: 'Men who manage treaties must give fair words', he pronounced, and he guessed that Breadalbane had indeed gone somewhat further than he should have. But he was more concerned to turn a temporary truce into a lasting one than to enquire how it had been arrived at.

In this he was undoubtedly supported by Queen Mary. In William's absence in Flanders she was asked to pass sentence on the first culprits to break the truce since the signing of the Treaty. They were men from Appin and Glencoe who had attacked a provision boat as it headed for Fort William. No one was killed but several clansmen were captured, including Alasdair Og, MacIain's younger son. The Privy Council asked Mary what she wished done with the troublemakers, and she promptly gave orders that they should be released. Nothing was to be allowed to impede the progress towards a settlement.

The next step was taken by William himself. On 17th August, in Flanders, he signed an order which contained a far-reaching promise – and a threat. It required those in rebellion to take a permanent and binding oath of allegiance to him before 1st January 1692, in return for which the Crown would be prepared to buy out the old feudal superiorities 'which are the subject of all these debates and animosities'. This was Tarbat's plan, and it was signed by the King. But by the time it had been posted on market crosses throughout Scotland, the message had been drastically simplified. There was no mention of the promises. Only the threat remained. Unless the oath were sworn within the time given, 'in presence of the Lords of our Privy Council – or the sheriff – or their deputies –

of the respective shires where any of the said persons live', those holding out would be punished by the full severity of the law. Little was offered in exchange for loyalty. And the time allowed was now only four months.

In the meantime the chiefs had begun to lose faith in Breadalbane's promises of money. Even some of his own friends suspected that he might have pocketed it himself; when the Earl of Nottingham tactfully enquired what had happened to it, he wrote: 'My Lord, the Highlands are quiet, the money is spent and that is the best way of accounting among friends'. Later he was to claim that the Highlanders had vacillated for so long he had returned the money to the Treasury, and it is reasonably certain that it could not have left London without the Government's knowledge.

No chief was prepared to sign any oath at all until word had come from King James. Messengers had left for Paris in August to ask him whether he was now prepared to release his followers. The mission had been entrusted to two men, Sir George Barclay and a young major, Duncan Menzies of Fornooth, but time was not on their side. Since their journey was anything but official, they had to leave the country secretly, travel to Paris, secure James's signature, return, and then see that the response was carried to every clan, however remote. If James had acted promptly, there would have been time for all this. But he had throughout his life found decisions hard to take, and now again he hesitated.

As autumn passed into winter in the Highlands there was still no word from France. In Glencoe, as elsewhere, the cattle were brought in from the shielings, and the people began to prepare for the hard days ahead. There was snow in November on the heights of the Aonach Eagach, and on Bidean nam Bian hard frosts suggested the winter might be a long one.

It is reasonable to assume that as Alasdair MacIain and his people celebrated the Feast of Samhain that November of 1691 they were more concerned with the fitness of their cattle than the threat of the Government's redcoats. At least one of Glencoe's tacksmen, John MacDonald of Achtriochtan, had Colonel Hill's letter of protection in his pocket, and Hill was trusted. They had been assured by Lochiel and Keppoch that messengers would soon be in Scotland bringing word one way or the other from Paris; the deadline of the year's end still seemed comfortably remote.

But, far from the Highlands, in the chambers of Kensington Palace in London, a plan was already beginning to take shape which was soon to shatter that sense of security.

Overleaf: The Geàrr Aonach and the Aonach Dubh, two of the Three Sisters, from the north-east

77

6

'TO MAUL THEM IN THE LONG COLD NIGHTS'

BY background and by temperament Sir John Dalrymple, the Master of Stair, was the perfect *éminence grise*. He understood the mood and inclinations of his king and could judge to a nicety when to press his own interests and when to stand back. Since his political ambitions accorded perfectly with William's, he had become a favoured minister at Court, with rooms in Kensington Palace and ready access to the royal chambers. He was widely recognised as one of the cleverest men in the kingdom.

His roots lay in Lowland Scotland. The Dalrymples had been thrifty farmers and lairds of some standing in Ayrshire since the 14th century. It was John Dalrymple's father, Sir James, who first rose to a position of influence by way, first of an academic post as Professor of Logic at Glasgow University, and then of a legal career, becoming Lord President of the Council in Edinburgh and one of the most celebrated writers of his time on Scots law. He still ranks today as one of Scotland's greatest lawyers.

Sir James was a remarkable survivor. A Royalist, he was nevertheless appointed a judge under Cromwell, and was knighted at the Restoration by Charles II. A Protestant with strong Presbyterian leanings, he stood up to the Catholic James II, refused to swear the Test Act, and left, with nice timing, for Holland, to join a more congenial monarch, William of Orange. He was therefore with William when he landed in Torbay in 1688 to claim the throne, and was raised to the peerage in 1690 as Viscount Stair. His son, in the Scottish tradition, became the Master of Stair.

These manoeuvrings won Sir James many enemies. 'The slippery Stair goes unstraight . . .' ran one lampoon, and the Dalrymple family became the butt of much malicious gossip in Scotland. Sir James's wife Margaret, a lady of strength and determination, who ran her husband's estates, was widely suspected by her neighbours of being a witch. Her daughter Janet, who may have been an epileptic, was the inspiration for Sir Walter Scott's *The Bride of Lammermoor*. She is said to have been persuaded by her mother to abandon the man she loved to marry a richer suitor, and to have met a terrible fate on her wedding night. What actually happened in the bridal chamber was a matter for fevered speculation. Either the bridegroom, on learning of her true feelings, stabbed her. Or she stabbed him and then went mad. Or else Janet's jilted lover climbed into the bedroom *via* a balcony and wreaked revenge on her husband. The story which gained the widest currency had the couple locked in their room by Janet's scheming mother. The night was filled with terrible screams and groans, and next day the bridegroom was found gibbering insanely in the fireplace while Janet lay on the bridal bed, drenched in blood.

The facts somewhat hamper the story. Janet did die young, just one month after her wedding, but her husband lived on in good health until he was killed by a fall from his horse 13 years later. There is no doubt, however, that there was something about the Dalrymple family which fed these dark rumours, and talk of a family curse persisted long afterwards. It was encouraged later by a tragic accident: one of Sir James's grandsons accidentally shot his brother with a pistol. The Devil hung around the family, muttered the locals, and a popular piece of doggerel ran:

It's not Stair's bairnes alone Nick doth infest
His children's children lykewise are possest.

Sir James's eldest son, John, was quite untouched by this idle gossip. The Master of Stair presented an appearance, like his father, of 'a perfectly calm and passionless' man, though he was harsh in language and capable of a brand of invective that won him few close friends. But, as events were to show, he was also subject to strong and sometimes irrational emotions, which he kept hidden behind a bland exterior.

His attitude towards his fellow human beings seemed all too often one of thinly-disguised contempt. His portrait shows a handsome, sensuous face; the heavy-lidded eyes are at once complacent and wary. There is, however, a trace of humour around the lips, and indeed his friends insisted that he was, in private, a good-natured companion, witty, well-read, and a great puncturer of other peoples' pomposity.

He had no respect for petty conventions. His wife, Elizabeth Dundas, had been abducted and raped by a disappointed lover, but neither the scandal, nor the loss of Elizabeth's virginity, troubled him, and Elizabeth went on to bear him nine children, and help run the family estates in Ayrshire and the fine house at Newliston near Edinburgh which had been part of her dowry.

Stair's career was less smooth than that of his father. Rising to the post of Lord Advocate under James II, he stayed on in Scotland when his father fled to Holland and was twice thrown into prison by Viscount Dundee, who believed him to be an ardent Presbyterian. In fact his religious views were in favour of tolerance, but that did not save him from three months in the Tolbooth and a large fine. He suffered 'from the original sin of his presbyterian father', he told friends philosophically.

When William of Orange landed in England and claimed the throne, Dalrymple moved smoothly to his side, finding himself, as one of his biographers noted, 'in an element that suited him, steering his bark on the troubled waters so as to place it on the crest of the incoming wave'. The next year, at the age of 41, he was one of the three commissioners who offered the Crown of Scotland to William in Whitehall. He did so with the conviction that union with England was the only logical future for his country. He believed that the union would encourage progress, that Scotland would benefit from the peace and stability which a strong government could offer, and that William III's revolution was a turning-point in history which Scotland should not ignore.

The obstacles that stood in the way were, he believed, rooted in the old Scotland and its outdated loyalties. He detested extremism, whether it be the Presbyterian Convenanters from his own part of the south-west, whom he once accused of 'attracting the idle, debauching the curious and harbouring criminals', or the Jacobites, whom he referred to derisively as the 'Killycrankies'.

But in the end it was the Highland clans which represented, to him, all that was backward, divisive and dangerous – a constant threat to the settled Lowlander and an affront to the dignity of modern Scotland. Holding them back imposed an intolerable

Above: The River Etive – an
escape route unguarded

strain on resources which were badly needed elsewhere, and their
loyalty to that indecisive and dissolute monarch, James, was
simple treason.

Stair knew little at first hand of conditions in the Highlands, but
what he knew he disliked. It was a subject on which he could not be
dispassionate. The Highlanders were savages, their customs barbarous, their dress absurd. Writing in 1690 to the Secretary of
State Lord Melville, he expressed a bizarre thought. 'In winter', he
wrote, 'the Highlanders cannot stay together, their garb render-
ing them incapable of remaining in the fields in the frost and snow,
nor can they scamper to the hills. The Lowlanders, being clothed,
can endure more cold in winter.' It was a remark based on ignorance, but it was to recur frequently in his letters. It would have
sinister implications for Glencoe two years later.

In January 1691 Stair became joint Secretary of State for Scotland with Melville. By the autumn Melville had been forced out
and the office was Stair's alone. Such was his favoured status that
Macaulay was later to refer to him as 'Prime Minister of Scotland'.
He divided his time between the King's military camp in Flanders
and his warm panelled rooms in Kensington Palace, from where he
could look down over the new Dutch garden being created in front
of the west wing, and ponder on the Scottish matters which now
seemed to him to be coming to a head.

There were two views about what should be done, and they were
incompatible. One, firmly held by the new Commander-in-Chief in
Scotland, Sir Thomas Livingstone, eager for success and not yet

83

40, was a military one, inherited from his predecessor, General Mackay. Swift, punitive action by well-trained foot-soldiers against the more intransigent clans would, he believed, achieve more in a matter of weeks than all the haggling over money or terms had ever done. He had suggested blowing up the mighty castle which Glengarry was fortifying between Fort William and Inverness, and had asked for an assault on the Lochaber clans, including the MacDonalds of Keppoch and Glencoe and the Stewarts of Appin. Both suggestions had been, sensibly and discreetly, ignored by Colonel Hill. The forces at his disposal were, he knew, incapable of such a strategy: they were inadequate in number, under-equipped and low on morale.

The other view was that the Highlanders could be persuaded to submit, or, as Hill put it, 'to sit quiet that the King's affairs may not be interrupted'. For the moment, Breadalbane's money scheme seemed to offer the best chance of success, and in that summer of 1691 Stair had been content to leave matters in his hands. Livingstone's proposals seemed simply to mean more expense and to offer limited prospects of success. He preferred the idea of a fixed sum of money and a signed treaty. He was, after all a pragmatist, and, as he wrote to Breadalbane:

'I hope your lordship shall not only keep them [the clans] from giving any offence, but bring them to take the allegiance which they ought to do very cheerfully, for their lives and fortunes they have from their Majesties'.

It is likely that Stair, a man of fine political judgment, knew precisely how far he could trust Breadalbane. He may have assured him of the King's confidence in him, and flattered him in Flanders when he came over to report on the Achallader meeting, but he must have been aware that Breadalbane might be playing a double game. Breadalbane's value, however, was that he knew the Highlands and could report at first hand on the mood and dispositions of the clans. Unlike the simple military mind, he had a grasp of what could and could not be realistically achieved. If peaceful means failed, then Breadalbane would provide ideal intelligence on the best way of exacting reprisals.

These would depend heavily on the army, which numbered some 6,500 soldiers in Scotland: 1,500 cavalry and 5,000 infantry. The latter consisted of six regiments, of which two were to be involved directly in the events to come. One was the Earl of Argyll's, the other Hill's own. Argyll had raised his regiment two years earlier from among his own clansmen, and had armed and equipped it himself. It consisted of 840 men, divided into 13 companies, recruited in Argyll and officered mainly by Campbell gentry. Trained by a Lowlander, Lieutenant Jackson, and by Major Robert Duncanson, a professional soldier from Stirling, it numbered among its more junior company commanders one Robert Campbell of Glenlyon, picking up a military career at the advanced age of 59 to help pay off his crippling debts.

In essence it was a Campbell regiment from top to bottom. The names on its muster rolls are those of Campbells, their allies and mercenaries, and though its loyalty was first to the Government, it was imbued with the spirit of a clan army. Indeed, its first action had been in the Earl of Argyll's endless war of attrition against the Macleans: a harrying battle on the island of Mull, where men called up in the service of the King, fought out a Campbell feud. They were armed like an English regiment, with pikes, muskets and the new bayonets, which could be clipped onto the barrel rather than plugged into the muzzle; but when they fought on Mull they charged in the name of Campbell. As soldiers and as clansmen they had no love for any MacDonalds.

The regiment was, at least while Argyll was financing it himself, well equipped and superbly turned out. 'I can assure your lordship', Argyll wrote to Melville, 'scarce any new regiment can be in better order than mine.' Hill's, by contrast, was ill-equipped and unhappy. The garrison at Fort William, which overlooked acres of swampland, was a damp, unhealthy place, and the death rate was monotonously high. Though Hill, assisted by John Forbes, now promoted to major, did as much as he could to hold his regiment together, he himself was in poor health most of the time.

In the late summer of 1691, Hill was given a new deputy-governor. He was Lieutenant-Colonel James Hamilton, a man who had seen service in Ireland, and whose attitude towards the Highlanders was as aggressive as Hill's was accommodating. Hamilton professed himself eager to take strong military action against the clans 'for reducing them to better manners'. Hill appears to have disliked and distrusted him, preferring the company of Forbes. This may have been because Hamilton had a more powerful patron than Hill's political masters in Edinburgh. The Master of Stair himself, by-passing Hill, wrote several letters direct to Hamilton which suggest that he was looking to him rather than to Hill to carry out the next stage of his Highland strategy.

By October, though some of the minor clansmen had reported to Hill that they were ready to take the oath, none of the chiefs had shown any sign of submission, and Stair was growing impatient. From all he could gather, the most openly defiant was still Glengarry, who flaunted his Jacobite sympathies, and Stair wrote angrily to Breadalbane suggesting that they should 'pull down Glengarry's nest' and convert it into a military post.

Other clan chiefs were almost as intransigent, and Breadalbane railed at them in a letter to one of his chamberlains in Glenorchy: 'They are ruined and abused with lies that children of ten years of age could not believe, and they talk as if they were to give terms and not to receive them; but they will find that a great mistake in a few weeks, notwithstanding any endeavours to the contrary.'

This letter contains the first hint that thoughts in London were now beginning to turn seriously to reprisal. On 1st December 1691, from his rooms in Kensington Palace, Stair began setting out, in a series of letters of growing ferocity, the plans he was beginning to refine for a final solution to the Highland problem. He had already chosen his instrument. The first of these letters was not to his Commander-in-Chief, nor to the Governor of Fort William, but to Lieutenant-Colonel Hamilton. It shows a degree of warmth surprising between a great minister and an officer of foot, and it suggests that Stair knew of some shadow over Hamilton's background which might be used against him if necessary:

'Yours of the 13th and 17th came to my hands both together . . . I do again assure you, the maintenance and provision of that garrison in Fort William, shall be always, and hath been my particular care. I do not consider the lapses of single persons, so as to make me do harm to what I do know to be their Majesties service. I am very glade you are there. And you shall see that my way is not so partiall, or to mind nothing but my own friends and interest. The publick shall always be first with me. And therefore, though I had never the good fortune to be acquainted with you, yet you shall find me as ready to do you justice, as if you were my nearest relation. You need not care that at present you are not to kiss the Kings hand. He wants not a just character of you. It may be shortly wee may have use of your garrison, for the winter time is the only season in which wee are sure the Highlanders cannot escape us, nor carry their wives, bairnes, and cattle to the mountaines. The Clan Donald is generally popish. Since the King hath to demonstration shown his exception, I am content that Clan doth except it selfe. I think Glengarry's estate will maintain a garison, to be a middle step betwixt yours and Inverness, which perhaps is more advantageous than his famed submission. And I well know that neither he, Keppoch, Appine, Lochiell, nor some Chiftanes, can well sleep, being within the reach of a good nights march of your garrison. Believe me I am, Sir, your very humble Servant, Sic subitur, Jo. Dalrymple.'

The seeds of a plan, discussed so far in general terms, but bearing the mark of Stair's fixed idea that the Highlanders were vulnerable in winter, had been sown. The next day Stair wrote more explicitly to Breadalbane. It was a long letter, full of the kind of subtle reassurances about Breadalbane's position at Court which could only have made that noble Lord profoundly uneasy; but in the course of it Stair gave him this information:

'Lt. Col. Hamilton is a discreet man; you may make use of him. I should be glad to find, before you get any positive order, that your business is done, for shortly we will conclude a resolution for the winter campaign. I do not fail to take notice of the frankness of your offer to assist. I think the Clan Donell must be rooted out, and Lochiel. Leave the M'Leans to Argyll . . . Now all stops, and no more money from England to entertain them. God knows whether the 12,000 sterling had been better employed to settle the Highlands or to ravage them; but, since we will make them desperate, I think we should root them out before they can get that help they depend on. Their doing, after they get K.J. [King James's] allowance, is worse than their obstinacy, for these who lay down their arms at his command will take them up at his warrant. Be assured no papist will be exempted from this oath of allegiance . . . My Lord, adieu.'

It is perhaps Stair's misfortune that his letters have survived, meticulously copied, to record his eloquent rancour, while Breadalbane's replies are unavailable. But it was not a one-sided correspondence, and there is no evidence that Breadalbane for his part was urging restraint.

Next day, on 3rd December, Stair wrote again to Breadalbane. His patience, he said, was at an end. The haggling over money, the

talk of buying out Argyll's feudal rights, all these were prevarications; either the rebels should take the oath or be punished:

'By the next I expect to hear either these people are come to your hand, or else your scheme for mauling them; for it will not delay . . . I am not charged as to the expediency of doing things by the easiest means, and at leisure, but the madness of these people, and their ungratefulness to you, makes me plainly see there is no reckoning on them; but *delenda est Carthago* . . . therefore look on and you shall be satisfied of your revenge.'

The Latin phrase is from Plutarch's life of Cato – 'Carthage must be destroyed' – but the sentiments are Stair's own; his reference to 'your scheme' shows that Breadalbane was actively suggesting a strategy for reprisal. On the same day Stair repeated his thoughts in a letter to Hamilton:

'I am satisfied these people are equally and unthinking, who do not accept what's never again in their offer. And since the government cannot oblige them, it's obliged to receive some of them to weaken and frighten the rest. The M'Donalds will fall in this net. That's the only popish clan in the kingdom and it will be popular to take severe course with them. Let me hear from you with the first whether you think that this is the proper season to maul them in the long cold nights . . .'

Nothing in the Highlands that December seemed to justify these murderous intentions. All was quiet. The clans waited still for word from James in his exiled court at St Germain. Three months had been allowed to go by, and time was now pressing if his release were to reach them before the deadline of 1st January 1692. Yet it was not until 12th December 1691 that that irresolute monarch-in-exile could persuade himself to agree. On that day he signed an order, to be carried back by Major Menzies, giving leave to the clans who had supported him so loyally 'to do what may be most for their own and your safety'. By delaying so long James had fatally compromised their chances of signing the oath in time. He must have known that in winter it would be perhaps three weeks before word could be brought by Menzies to Edinburgh, and thence spread to each of the clans. Yet he had allowed a bare 19 days.

Duncan Menzies knew exactly what was at stake and did his best to fulfil his duty. He took nine days to get to Edinburgh from Paris, and by the time he arrived he was in a state of exhaustion. Nevertheless, he left again next day, on 22nd December, and reached his home in Perthshire, four miles from Dunkeld, where he collapsed. From there, he sent messengers out to Lochaber and beyond. Menzies' urgent news was repeated by letters sent direct from Edinburgh by Breadalbane's chamberlain, Alexander Campbell of Barcaldine. Breadalbane himself had by now posted south to London to keep in touch with the accelerating pace of events.

On 28th December Ewen Cameron of Lochiel received the message and immediately set out for Inveraray, the nearest town where he would find a sheriff entitled to administer the oath. Already, however, there were soldiers on the move. Several companies had been posted north from Perth, Stirling, Dundee and Aberdeen, and on 29th December, on Stair's orders, 800 men from the Earl of Argyll's regiment marched north from Inveraray.

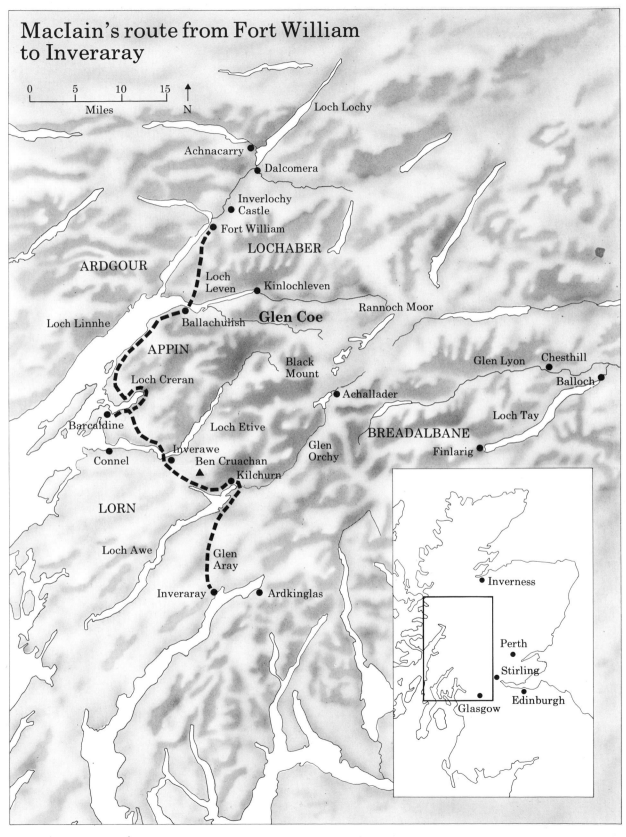

MacIain's route from Fort William to Inveraray

0 5 10 15
Miles

N

Loch Lochy

Achnacarry

Dalcomera

Inverlochy Castle

Fort William

LOCHABER

ARDGOUR

Loch Leven

Kinlochleven

Rannoch Moor

Glen Coe

Loch Linnhe

Ballachulish

APPIN

Black Mount

Glen Lyon

Chesthill

Balloch

Loch Creran

Achallader

Barcaldine

Loch Etive

Loch Tay

BREADALBANE

Connel

Inverawe

Ben Cruachan

Kilchurn

Glen Orchy

Finlarig

LORN

Loch Awe

Glen Aray

Inveraray

Ardkinglas

Inverness

Perth

Stirling

Glasgow

Edinburgh

91

When precisely word of King James's release came to Glencoe is not known, but it may have been on that very day, 29th December. By then the weather had turned, and it was snowing heavily, with great gusts of wind driving snow flurries through the icy passes and piling them up in drifts.

MacIain set out on a sturdy garron pony with two or three retainers. But instead of heading south for Inveraray he turned north-east towards Fort William. Why he did so is unclear. He may not have fully understood that the oath had to be taken 'in the presence of the Sheriffs or their deputies', and that Hill, even though he was the military governor who had already given some of MacIain's kinsmen letters of protection, was not empowered to do the same for him. Or perhaps he simply could not, at this late stage, bring himself to submit so publicly to a Campbell at the stronghold of Inveraray, where he himself had been so recently a prisoner. Whatever the reason, it was a fatal mistake.

MacIain arrived late that day, and walked into Colonel Hill's room at the barracks of Fort William. There he asked the Governor to administer the oath so that he and his people could receive King William's indemnity.

John Hill must, at that moment, have experienced mixed feelings as this towering figure stood before him. MacIain, the proudest of chiefs, had finally decided to submit, and that was a cause for enormous relief. But he had left it dangerously late, and that must have irritated him and filled him with foreboding. For Hill knew by now that Hamilton had been in correspondence with Stair behind his back and that plans had been laid which went far beyond his own conception of how the Highlanders should be treated. The chief of a small clan would be specially vulnerable.

Hill may well have reproached MacIain for leaving the oath until the last possible moment, but in the end he relented, and wrote out a letter to the Sheriff of Argyll, Sir Colin Campbell of Ardkinglas, asking him to receive MacIain as 'a lost sheep'.

Hill knew Sir Colin to be an honest man who was likely to give MacIain the benefit of the doubt, despite the fact that his had been one of the Campbell estates ravaged six years earlier in the Atholl raid. He handed MacIain the letter and told him to ride as hard as possible for Inveraray. Both men must have known that it would, at best, be a close-run thing. The distance to Inveraray from Fort William as the crow flies is barely 40 miles. But the weather would force MacIain to take the long coast road, adding 20 miles to the distance.

With the snow still driving from the north-west, the little party set off along the shore of Loch Linnhe and crossed the narrows of Loch Leven by the ferry at Ballachulish. They passed barely half a mile from MacIain's house at Carnoch, but time was too pressing for them to stop. One of the ghillies was dispatched to explain what had happened.

The quickest way south, if the weather had been good, would have been up the Laroch glen, and on between Beinn Bheithir (Ben Vair) and Meall Mór on the western flank of Glencoe. That would have led quickly to Glen Creran and the ferry at Connel. But in that storm even a stag would have found the route impassable. Instead MacIain and his men turned right and followed the shore line of Loch Linnhe towards Appin.

By the next day, bitterly cold and lashed by the wind, they had reached Loch Creran, ready to strike south towards Inverawe. Their chances of reaching Inveraray before the year ran out were rapidly fading, but they struggled on, heads bowed before the wind, their plaids drenched and icy. Suddenly they were challenged. A party of red-coated soldiers, men of Argyll's regiment, stood before them on the lochside track, armed with muskets, demanding to know their business. MacIain pulled Hill's letter from his pocket to show he had been given protection. But the soldiers refused to accept it. Instead they hurried the small and bedraggled party westwards along the track to Barcaldine castle, a Campbell stronghold, where Captain Thomas Drummond had halted, with a small detachment of grenadiers, on his way north to Fort William. It was a disastrous piece of bad luck. Drummond read Hill's letter but refused to allow MacIain and his men to go. Instead he held them at Barcaldine for 24 hours – a day that finally cost them their last chance of reaching Inveraray on time.

By the time they were released and on their way south, the old year was gone. They rested on the night of 1st January 1692 in a deserted shieling within sight of Ben Cruachan, then dropped down the final slopes of Glen Aray and stumbled into Inveraray itself, two days behind their deadline.

There they were given bad news. Sir Colin Campbell of Ardkinglas was not there. He had gone to spend Hogmanay with relations and had been delayed by the storm.

The next three days must have been miserable for the Glencoe men, alone in a hostile town where New Year revelry was still in spate and the sight of a MacDonald might well have provoked an explosive brawl. They stayed indoors in a tiny inn, while MacIain reflected on the use his enemies might make of this disastrous delay. On 5th January Sir Colin returned, and met MacIain at the Court House. His reputation was that of a fair man, but he saw no immediate reason why MacIain's excuses should be accepted. He read Hill's letter, with its plea that 'it was good to bring in a lost sheep at any time' and its explanation that MacIain had 'slipt some days, out of ignorance', but he refused at first to change his mind. The King's proclamation had been issued five months ago, and it was absurd to plead misunderstandings or bad weather for so late an arrival.

This brusque refusal finally broke the old man's resistance. Exhausted by the strain of his journey and the fear of what he and his people might now face at the hands of a vengeful government, MacIain wept. Pride and defiance were forgotten as he pleaded with Ardkinglas to relent. He would bring every grown member of his clan in, if necessary, to take the oath, and if any of them refused they might be imprisoned, or sent to Flanders to serve as soldiers in the King's army.

Perhaps it was the humiliation of this once proud chief, his face stained with tears as he begged for mercy on behalf of his people, that moved Ardkinglas finally to sympathy. He ordered MacIain to report back to him the following day, when he would accept the

oath, late though it was, and send it to Edinburgh by messenger.

It was, therefore, on 6th January that the oath of allegiance to William and Mary was sworn by the Chief of Glencoe, and dispatched with a letter of explanation to the Sheriff-Clerk of Argyll, Colin Campbell of Dressalch, who was at that time in Edinburgh. The letter requested him to pass MacIain's oath on directly to the Privy Council.

It is clear that Ardkinglas, having relented, was determined that the lateness of MacIain's submission should not be held against him, and it confirms his reputation for fairness. He enclosed with his letter a copy of Hill's original request asking him to receive 'the lost sheep of Glencoe'; he asked the Sheriff-Clerk to let him know what the Council's decision would be; and he wrote to Hill assuring him that he had accepted MacIain's oath.

The letters from Ardkinglas reached Colin Campbell some six days later. It seems that none of the lawyers who considered the matter in Edinburgh that January were eager to take the responsibility of deciding whether to record the oath or not. The fact that they were mostly Campbells – as so many of the legal profession were – was probably less important than their anxiety not to circumvent the strict letter of the law. Colin Campbell consulted a colleague, John Campbell, and both talked to another Campbell, Lord Aberuchill. They canvassed the views privately of various privy councillors, including the most influential of them all, the Viscount Stair, now 72, father of the Master of Stair. Their overwhelming opinion was the law should stand: MacIain was too late.

Ardkinglas's entreaty that the request should be laid before the Privy Council as a whole was ignored. Acting on the private views of a few of its members, Campbell of Dressalch scored out MacIain's name from the list, though later, when that document became a crucial piece of evidence, it was possible to discern that the signature had once been there, 'fairly writen and not dashed . . . bearing how earnest Glencoe was to take the oath of allegiance'.

Meanwhile MacIain himself, with his faithful ghillies, was on the road back to Glencoe with a lighter heart than when he had last been on it. The weather had lifted and the snow was melting as they skirted the Black Mount and came in below the Buachaille Etive Mór. Gathering his people together, he announced that the oath of allegiance had been sworn and he had made his peace with Their Majesties. The MacDonalds of Glencoe could now live peaceably under the Government. He had given his word that there would be no trouble and he warned that it was now a matter of honour that they should respect the oath that he, the MacIain, had sworn in Inveraray.

Opposite: The River Coe beneath Gearr Aonach

Overleaf: The Three Sisters overlooking Achtriochtan, where much of the slaughter took place

7

'A GREAT WORK
OF
CHARITY'

ON the evening of 7th January 1692, the Earl of Breadalbane entertained two guests to dinner at his London house. The Master of Stair and the Earl of Argyll had come to discuss what Stair referred to as 'the Highland business'. News from Scotland was still incomplete, but it seemed clear that several of the clan chiefs had either failed to take the oath on time or had postponed it to the last possible moment as a deliberate act of defiance.

Of the three men, Breadalbane was the least certain about what should now be done. He still clung hopefully to his scheme for bribing the clans, though Stair had made it clear that this was now an idea of the past. Recently Breadalbane had begun, in his letters north, to distance himself from the events to come. 'All methods have been ordered before I came here for that which will shortly be put into execution,' he wrote to his chamberlain, Campbell of Barcaldine. 'I haven't meddled in it, measures were agreed on before I came.' But he knew enough. It was, after all, he who had first proposed a plan for military action.

Argyll was closer to the heart of the affair. His regiment was to be the main instrument for action, and his soldiers had only just been sent north to Fort William. He had seen much of Stair in the past few weeks and enjoyed his confidence, though how much detailed information he had been given is uncertain.

As for Stair himself, he knew exactly what was intended. He had set out his orders only that morning to Sir Thomas Livingstone and despatched them north with a covering letter:

'The orders may be with you by a flying pacquet almost as this comes to your hands, therefore I do intreat you to be providing what will be necessary for your expedition. You know in generall that these troops posted at Inverness and Inverlochy will be ordered to take in the house of Invergarry, and to destroy intirely the country of Lochaber, Lochiell's lands, Keppoch's, Glengaries, Appine and Glencoe. If there be any opposition, then the troops will need to joyne; if not they may act separately, which will make the work the shorter. I assure you their power shall be full enough, and I hope the soldiers will not trouble the Government with prisoners . . . It's true, it's a rigid season for the souldiers to work, but it's the only time that they cannot escape you; for human constitution cannot endure long out of houses.'

The scheme was absurdly ambitious. How much of it Stair discussed that evening at the dinner table we do not know. Perhaps, since Cameron of Lochiel was related to Breadalbane, he spared him the details. He was fond of referring to Lochiel as 'your doited cousin' (your demented cousin), but he might have hesitated to tell his host exactly how that cousin was now to be treated. Certainly Breadalbane, writing to Lochiel two days later, said nothing of it.

On the following day, 8th January, news from Scotland had begun to harden – though it was partly inaccurate. Lochiel had submitted, it appeared, as had the chiefs of McNaughton, Appin, Keppoch and Glencoe. Others still held out, including Glengarry, Maclean and Clanranald. Stair wrote immediately to Livingstone telling him that the plan still stood, though its scope would now inevitably have to be restricted:

'There are so many come in, which breaks the wicked bond and knot, that these who remain are not able to oppose, and their Chiftans being all papists, it's well the revenge falls there. For my part I could have wished the MacDonalds had not divided, and I am sorry Keppoch and M'Kean of Glencoe are safe.'

The great act of retribution he had planned was now reduced in scale. It meant taking Glengarry's fort, an exercise he knew would be long and costly; Argyll would be authorised to pursue his campaign against the Macleans; and a military assault on the far-flung lands of Clanranald, MacDonalds of Sleat, Stewarts of Appin and others to the west would be launched. But this, Stair realised, would be expensive, long-drawn-out, and quite possibly ineffective. If only the Keppoch MacDonalds had held out, or Glencoe, in its bottled-up valley, things would have been easier.

That weekend, however, the orders were drawn up and signed by King William at the top and bottom, a mark of the special importance he attached to them. They were orders of Fire and Sword in the traditional manner, authorising Livingstone to 'burn their houses, seize or destroy their goods or cattle, plenishing or clothes, and to cut off the men'. But there was more than a hint of compromise running through the document. The leaders were to be captured and required to take the oath rather than to be killed; lesser folk would be ordered to surrender their arms and swear allegiance, in which case they must not be plundered; the troops should forage 'with the greatest ease and tenderness to the country that you can'. It was to be, in fact, a gesture of harshness rather than an act of destruction.

Stair caught the King's drift admirably. Dictating a letter to accompany the orders to Livingstone on the evening of 11th January, he wrote: 'I am much concerned for the poor comonalty . . . it would be hard to take the legall advantage of them if they be willing to submit, take oathes, and deliver their armes.' He suggested that if they did so, the lease on their lands might be paid directly to the army to fund the garrisons.

This was poor stuff compared to what might have been. 'I have no great kindness to Keppoch nor Glencoe,' he mused, 'and it's well that their people are in mercy . . .'

Just then Stair was interrupted at his work. He had a visitor. It was Argyll with the latest word from the Highlands, and when Stair resumed his letter there was an important addition:

'Just now my Lord Argile tells me that Glenco hath not taken the oaths, at which I rejoice, it's a great work of charity to be exact in rooting out that damnable sept, the worst in all the Highlands'.

Argyll had heard direct from Ardkinglas the news that MacIain had been late, and the timing of his message weighted the scale against Glencoe. But did Argyll give Stair a complete report? The question is critical in assessing his share of responsibility for the events to come. Ardkinglas had, after all, administered the oath to MacIain despite the fact that he had come in late. MacIain was therefore 'in mercy' and Ardkinglas must have informed Argyll of this. So either Stair was indeed told by Argyll, but ignored the saving clause; or Argyll chose deliberately to conceal it; or, which is equally possible, both men were fully aware of the circumstances and decided together that Glencoe should nevertheless be singled out for punishment.

It was the first time Stair's 'great work of charity' had been directed specifically against the Glencoe MacDonalds. Until then they had been recorded simply as one of several troublesome Lochaber clans. But over the next five days, as he consulted Argyll and Breadalbane further, the merits of making a bloody example of this single tribe of people, whose whole history, it was now clear to him, had been one of raiding, thieving and wanton barbarity, became ever stronger. Not least of the advantages was strategic. This little valley, so long regarded as a fortress, was also a trap, whose exits might be blocked so that no one inside could escape: a far more straightforward proposition than Glengarry's castle, which required artillery and provisions for a long siege.

Besides, word had now reached Stair that Glengarry had finally decided to take the oath. It was late – far later than MacIain's – but his offer was accepted with alacrity. On 16th January further orders were sent from the King to Livingstone, authorising him to accept the terms, to allow Glengarry's guests – the Jacobite officers, Buchan and Cannon – free passes to leave Scotland, and to accept the keys to his castle.

The final paragraph of William's orders contained one sentence. At a glance it might almost be read as an afterthought. But the document was signed at the top and bottom by the King, and it is inconceivable that Stair, who had composed it, should have failed to discuss its implication with him:

'If M'Kean of Glencoe and that tribe can be well separated from the rest, it will be a proper vindication of the publick justice to extirpate that sept of thieves.'

As the ink dried on the order William may have realised that the promises of justice and tolerance enshrined in his Declaration of Rights were about to be rescinded. The word extirpate means literally to 'root out'. In Scotland its use was familiar: it meant to punish, by burning crops, driving off cattle, killing any armed men who resisted. But it bore, too, a stronger interpretation, one more familiar, perhaps, to the 20th century than to the 17th. It meant 'to exterminate', and that is the sense in which it was finally to be taken. Stair himself undoubtedly meant no less.

The King's order was despatched to Colonel Hill as Governor of Fort William, and Stair's letters, sent the same day, show that he had consulted both Argyll and Breadalbane in refining the strategy which would now be employed. To Hill he wrote:

'I shall intreat you that for a just vengeance and publick example, the thieving tribe of Glencoe may be rooted out to purpose. The Earles of Argyle and Broadalban have promised that they shall have no retreat in their bounds. The passes to Rannoch would be secured . . .'

On the same day Stair wrote to the Marquis of Tweeddale: 'I am extremely glad that the murderer MacIain of Glencoe did not accept the benefit of the indemnity. I hope care will be taken to root out that thieving tribe.' There is no record that any of those to whom Stair confided his plans objected in the least to what he proposed.

Overleaf: Achtriochtan, looking north-west; the route down which Hamilton was to march

In Edinburgh Livingstone seized the chance for some proper military action with enthusiasm. He wrote to Lieutenant-Colonel Hamilton at Fort William:

'Sir, Since my last I understand that the Laird of Glenco, coming after the prefixed time, was not admitted to take the oath, which is very good news here, being that at Court it's wished he had not taken it, so that that thieving nest might be intirely rooted out, for the Secretary in three of his last letters hath made mention of him, and it is known at Court he has not taken it. So Sir, here is a fair occasion for you to show that your garrison serves for some use; and being that the orders are so positive from Court to me not to spare any of them that have not timely come in, as you may by the orders I sent to Your Col. I desire you would begin with Glenco and spair nothing which belongs to him, but do not trouble the Government with prisoners. I shall expect to hear what progress you have made in this and remain, Sir, Your humble servant, T. Livingston'.

Livingstone wrote directly to Hamilton, the deputy-governor, rather than Colonel Hill, his superior officer. Like Stair before him, he realised perhaps that Hill could not be relied on to pursue the matter with sufficient vigour, and that he might prove to be an unwilling participant in the scheme.

Hill, of course, was perfectly well aware that Glencoe had been singled out for punishment. Stair had made it clear to him in his last letter, and he had raised no objection. For one thing the orders were clear, and he was first and foremost a soldier. For another thing, Glencoe had flouted the King's orders and did after all deserve some firm reprimand.

Hill would not have objected to that. But he may not have known, or have been careful not to question too closely, the nature of the action proposed. Certainly Stair seems to have been conscious of the old man's sensibilities when he penned his final thoughts on the Glencoe matter on 30th January from Kensington Palace. In the middle of a long letter to Hill on broad strategy in the Highlands he let fall this sentence:

'Pray, when anything concerning Glenco is resolved, let it be secret and suddain, otherwayes the men will shift you and better not meddle with them than not to do it to purpose, to cutt off that nest of robbers who have fallen in the mercy of the law now when there is force and opportunity, whereby the King's justice will be as conspicuous and useful as his clemency to others. I apprehend the storme is so great that for sometime you can do little, but so soon as possible I know you will be at work, for these false people will do nothing, but as they see you in condition to do with them.'

Although Stair urged the need for surprise and stealth, the tone in this letter to Hill was coaxing, unlike his words to Livingstone, written on the same day:

'I am glad that Glencoe did not come in within the time prescribed. I hope what's done they may be in earnest, since the rest are not in condition to draw together to help. I think to harry their cattle or burn their houses is but to render them desperate, lawless men, to rob their neighbours; but I believe you will be satisfied it were a great advantage to the nation that thieving tribe were rooted out and cutt off. It must be quietly done, otherwise they will make shift for both the men and their cattle. Argile's detachment lies in Letrick well to assist the garrison to do all on a suddain.'

The business was now in hand. Stair's earlier instructions, together with the King's orders, had reached Edinburgh on 20th January. There they were collected by Major John Forbes, who broke the seals and sent them on before riding himself for Fort William. By the end of the month, even as Stair was composing his final thoughts on the subject, the arrangements were complete.

In the Highlands troops were everywhere on the move. Major Robert Duncanson had moved up with five companies of the Earl of Argyll's regiment – almost 400 men – to the north side of the ferry at Ballachulish. One of those companies was under the command of Captain Robert Campbell of Glenlyon, still attempting to pay off his obligations to his cousin Breadalbane on an officer's pay of eight shillings a day. A grenadier company was commanded by Captain Thomas Drummond, Duncanson's second in command, the man who had held up MacIain for those 24 fatal hours as he hurried south to take the oath at Inveraray.

In Fort William there were seven companies of Colonel Hill's regiment – nearly 500 men. But the man who was now to issue the crucial instructions as to how Glencoe should be taken was not Hill but his deputy, Hamilton.

On 1st February, two of Duncanson's companies, Glenlyon's and Drummond's, marched out from Ballachulish, led by Glenlyon. Drummond himself appears to have stayed behind, though he was to join his men later, after they had reached their destination in Glencoe. The snow-storms had died away and the waters of Loch Leven were calm under grey skies as the soldiers approached Glencoe along the shore road. They were seen by Major Forbes, riding north on the final leg of his journey from Edinburgh; since Forbes had read the orders which he had dispatched to Hill, he must have been aware of the expedition's purpose.

Word of approaching troops reached Glencoe ahead of them and spread the length of the valley. MacIain himself was informed, and he ordered his men to hide their weapons in peat-stacks or under stones on the hillside. There was, he believed, no real reason to fear Argyll's soldiers, for he had Hill's word that he was safe. But his people were nervous and suspicious, and it was natural to take precautions.

The soldiers, with their red coats, long waistcoats and grey breeks, hidden by greatcoats, their muskets or pikes slanted on their shoulders, and their knapsacks slung behind them, swung south towards Invercoe and halted before the mouth of the glen.

MacIain sent his elder son John, with about 20 men, to meet them and ask them their business. One of Glenlyon's lieutenants, John Lindsay, went forward to talk. Glenlyon himself waited at the head of his column.

He was a striking figure. Tall, with straw-coloured hair and the florid complexion of a man who stays much out of doors, or drinks too much, or both, Glenlyon at 60 was still handsome, though there was a touch of weakness round the mouth. It was only at close quarters that his face showed the signs of a lifetime's self-indulgence: his eyes had the glazed look of a man who relies too much on the bottle.

A drinker, a gambler, and a reckless money-spender incapable of looking after his own affairs, he had lost all his lands in Glenlyon except for one small estate, which was now held in his wife's name. He had inherited debts from his grandfather, himself a gambling man, and had borrowed from most of his relations, particularly his cousin Breadalbane, in an effort to repay them.

As his creditors multiplied, so his gambling and mortgages increased. Nonetheless, he appears to have inspired affection and loyalty among his clansmen, for he led them on several raids to avenge some real or imagined slight, and in 1678 took them north on Breadalbane's famous raid into Caithness. Despite his debts he continued to live in the style of a great laird, building an extension to Meggernie Castle, the family seat where his great-grandfather, Mad Colin, had once hanged 36 MacDonalds. Glenlyon married late, but made up for it with 11 children – five boys and six girls.

By the time he was in his fifties Glenlyon was virtually destitute. Against the wishes of Breadalbane, and to the anguish of his tenants, he sold the long and beautiful valley his family had owned for generations, and Glen Lyon passed to the Murrays of Atholl. All that was left was the small estate of Chesthill. Breadalbane wrote in despair: 'He is an object of compassion when I see him, but when he is out of sight I could wish he had never been born.'

In 1689 his plight worsened when the MacDonalds of Keppoch and Glencoe raided through Glen Lyon on their way back from Killiecrankie. The Chesthill estate suffered with the rest, and in the winter of 1690 Glenlyon's family came close to starvation. Glenlyon cannot therefore have felt anything but bitterness towards the bandit clan which had finally ruined his land.

But he was familiar with Glencoe for another reason: he was actually related to the clan, through John MacDonald's younger brother, Alasdair Og. The genealogy is uncertain, but Alasdair's wife seems to have been a grand-daughter of Glenlyon's mother, a splendid lady called Jean Campbell, who was sister of the tenth Laird of Glenorchy, and Breadalbane's aunt. She had cut across clan barriers by marrying three times: first a Campbell of Glenlyon, then a MacGregor and lastly a Stewart of Appin, from whom Alasdair's wife was said to be descended. The relationship was close enough for Glenlyon to be referred to in Glencoe as an uncle.

It must therefore have been with mixed feelings that John McDonald studied this man who was both a Campbell and a relative, and was now bringing Argyll's soldiers into the glen. As John waited warily, Lieutenant Lindsay produced a letter, signed by Colonel Hill, which required Glencoe to offer the soldiers bed and board for a few days. No harm was intended, he said, it was simply a matter of billeting the soldiers and supplying them with food and shelter; it was a prerogative of the garrison commander at Fort William that he could quarter his soldiers on any civilian in the area if the need arose.

Glenlyon himself now came up to offer his own explanations and

to dissolve John's suspicions with hearty greetings. He apologised for the imposition, and explained that his companies had been detailed to mount an expedition against Glengarry's castle. The garrison at Fort William was overcrowded and they would require Glencoe's hospitality for a few days at the most. At the same time he had been ordered to collect two taxes, known as cess and hearth money, imposed by the Government two years earlier, which Glencoe, not surprisingly, had failed to pay.

Clearly John MacDonald had little choice but to offer Glenlyon his hand and walk back with him to MacIain's house at Carnoch. There the Chief of Glencoe himself shook hands with him and extended to him and his soldiers the hospitality of his people. It was mid-winter and the season had been a hard one, but there would be room and provisions enough.

The soldiers were dispersed throughout the glen, billeted by threes and fives depending on the size of their quarters. They crowded into the tiny, smoking houses which were to be their homes for the next 13 days, jostling for space with dogs, horses or cattle; conditions must have been appallingly cramped.

The muster rolls of Glenlyon's company, drawn up four months earlier, show that it had three officers, five non-commissioned officers, two drummers and 57 men. Since then there had been some changes among the officers. Apart from Glenlyon himself and Lieutenant Lindsay, there was a young ensign, John Lundie; the senior sergeant of the company was a Lowlander, Robert Barber; the privates were either Campbells or men whose names show that they came from Argyll, with a sprinkling of Lowlanders as well. Among Drummond's company of 68 officers and men, Lowland names predominated.

Sergeant Barber, with his party, was quartered with Mac-Donald of Achnacon, the senior tacksman, whose house was across the burn from Signal Rock. Lindsay and Lundie, with their men, were scattered further down the glen. Glenlyon himself chose the house of MacDonald of Inverrigan, between Carnoch and Achnacon. It is odd that he should not have stayed with MacIain himself, but there is some confusion as to whether the Chief of Glencoe was actually living in his winter quarters at Carnoch at this time or not. Some accounts insist that he had chosen to move to his summer house at Gleann-leac-na-muidhe, about a mile and a half off the glen to the west of Achnacon. Others believe that the real site of his residence was in the centre of the glen, east of Inverrigan, and that it was here that he and his wife were living.

It is certainly clear that Glenlyon did not care to accept his hospitality, and this may have indicated a guilty conscience. The decision of a man fond of good living to turn down the offer of the best house in Glencoe may well indicate that he found it impossible to live under the same roof as the friendly and likeable MacIain in the certain knowledge that he was there to murder him. There is no firm evidence, however, that Glenlyon had yet been told the ultimate purpose of his mission.

Over the next few days the MacDonalds and their guests slowly grew used to each other. The days were mild and pleasant, as they can be in the middle of a Highland winter. The snow disappeared from the floor of the glen, and while the soldiers drilled daily under Sergeant Barber, the men and women went about their winter tasks as usual. In the afternoon they played games together, running, wrestling, competing at archery, or at shinty, the fierce Gaelic hockey played with a curved stick and a round stone, common throughout the west Highlands.

In the evenings, round the fires, fortified by whisky and wine (the only supplies which the soldiers had brought with them) they told their stories and sang their songs. Some tact may have been necessary on both sides to censor the more offensive references to Campbell treachery or MacDonald slaughter, but there are no reports of any trouble during those winter nights. The Lowlanders among the soldiers, with their lack of Gaelic, would have found themselves outsiders on these occasions, but there was dancing, in which all could join, and the finer points of the *Piobaireachd* to be dutifully appreciated.

Every evening at Inverrigan, Glenlyon and the MacDonald gentry played cards and backgammon; since Glenlyon was an inveterate gambler, sums of money doubtless changed hands. Every morning Glenlyon walked over to the house of Alasdair Og and took the day's first nip of whisky with him and his wife before going off to inspect his men.

Not all the Glencoe folk took easily to the presence of the soldiers. Alasdair Og himself was far more suspicious about the real intentions of the Argyll men than his father or brother, and was to remain so to the end; his wife, too, was uneasy. Others voiced angry complaints at having to feed the extra bodies. They were all reassured by MacIain himself. He pointed out that the laws of hospitality laid obligations on guests as well as on hosts, and these could not be ignored. Once bread had been broken and a roof shared, there was a bond of friendship between the two. Besides, had he not sworn the Government's oath and been assured of the protection that went with it?

The troops were in Glencoe for 12 days before their orders arrived. The delay may have been because the weather was too mild for the planned operation. Or perhaps Colonel Hill, whose signature was needed, could not bring himself to take the final step. But towards the end of the second week in February the weather started to close in, with snow falling on the heights and the wind beginning to rise. Then, too, Stair's last letters, penned on 30th January, arrived – one to Livingstone in Inverness, one to Hill. There was no going back. 'Let it be secret and sudden', he insisted.

Hill now wrote an order to his deputy, Hamilton, which bears in its six short lines the signs of a man attempting to stay at arms' length from the action he was setting in motion:
'Sir, You are with four hundred of my regiment, and the four hundred of my Lord Argile's regiment, under the command of Major Duncanson, to march straight to Glenco, and there put in execution the orders you have received from the Commander in Chiefe. Given under my hand at Fort William, the 12th February 1692. Sic Subtur. Jo Hill.'

Hamilton immediately despatched a runner to Major Duncanson, who was still camped with his men on the north side of the

Right: Duncanson's despatch to Campbell of Glenlyon – 'You are to have a speciall care that the old fox and his sones doe upon no account escape your hands'

Ballachulish ferry. It is clear that Duncanson was familiar with the plan. The order from Hamilton was a formal expression of it:

'For Their Majesties' Service, for Major Robert Duncanson of the Earl of Argyll's Regiment. Fort William 12 February 1692. Sir, Pursuant to the Commander-in-Chiefe and my Colonell's orders to me for putting in execution the service against the rebells of Glenco, wherein you with that party of the Earl of Argile's Regiment now under your command are to be concerned. You are therefore to order your affairs so that you be at the several posts assigned to you by seven of the clock tomorrow morning, being Saturday, and fall in action with them, at which time I will endeavour to be with the party from this place at the post appointed them. It will be necessary the avenues minded by Lieutenant Campbell [this is Hamilton's error – it should of course be Captain Campbell] on the south side be secured, that the old fox nor none of his cubs get away. The orders are that none be spared, nor the government troubled with prisoners, which is all I have to say to you till then. Sir, your humble servant James Hamilton. Please to order a guard to secure the ferry and the boats there; and the boats must be all on this side the ferry after your men are over.'

This document would have reached Duncanson later that Friday in time for him to pen the third and most explicit of the three orders despatched in the course of the day. It is an order which explains precisely what is expected of Glenlyon, and it gives stern warning of the risks should he disobey. Whether Glenlyon knew in advance or not, there was no mistaking it now.

'You are hereby ordered to fall upon the Rebells, the McDonalds of Glenco, and putt all to the sword under seventy. You are to have a speciall care that the old fox and his sones doe upon no account escape your hands you are to secure all the avenues thatt no man escape. This you are to putt in execution att fyve of the clock precisely; and by that time, or verie shortly after it I'le strive to be att you with a stronger party: if I do not come to you at fyve, you are not to tarry for me, butt to fall on. This is by the Kings speciall command, for the good safty of the Country, that these miscreants be cutt off root and branch. See that this be putt in execution without feud or favour, else you may expect to be dealt with as one not true to King nor Government, nor a man fitt to carry Commissione in the King's Service. Expecting you will not faill in the fulfilling hereof, as you love your Selfe, I subscribe these with my hand att Balichulis, Feb 12, 1692, Ro. Duncanson. For ther Majies' Service. To Capt Robert Campbell of Glenlyon.'

The trap was set. Glenlyon, with his 120 men, would seal the escape routes on the southern flanks. Duncanson, with some 300 more soldiers, would move up to Invercoe at the mouth of the glen to stop up the way out to Loch Leven. And Hamilton, with another 400, would march from Fort William, over the Devil's Staircase, to close the passes to the south and east. The matter of disposing of some 500 men, women and children was thus in the hands of almost 1,000 armed men. But the timing meant that Hamilton would not be there for at least two hours after the action had begun. And even Duncanson, with a far shorter journey to make, had indicated that he might be late. The responsibility for the success of the operation was placed firmly on Glenlyon.

None of the senior officers appear to have protested openly, but the orders did not go unquestioned lower down the hierarchy. At some point, possibly back in Fort William that Friday when Hamilton's orders to march were given, two junior officers announced that they would refuse to take part. They were immediately arrested and sent south for court martial to Glasgow.

And later, in Glencoe itself, there would be others, ordinary soldiers, Highland or Lowland, who had grown fond of the families with whom they had lived now for 12 days. Some of them would find the brutality of their orders intolerable, and would do their best to avoid the responsibility of carrying them out.

Overleaf: 'Great stone of the glen, great is your right to be here. Yet if you but knew what would happen this night . . .' The view from the Devil's Staircase

113

8

'COLD, COLD THIS NIGHT'

Major Duncanson's orders arrived in Glencoe late that Friday evening, 12th February. By now it was freezing cold. The wind was blowing from the north and the snow was driving down the steep cliff-face of the Aonach Eagach. The only men visible outside the cottages were the soldiers of the watch, hunched in their great-coats. The rest were inside round blazing peat fires. At Inverrigan Glenlyon was at cards with the MacIain brothers, Alasdair and John. He was his usual ebullient self, his face flushed, his voice loud with drink. He had been invited the next evening to dine at the Chief's house with his two junior officers, Lieutenant Lindsay and Ensign Lundie, and he was looking forward to it.

The gambling was interrupted by Duncanson's runner, and the arrival from Ballachulish of Captain Drummond, Glenlyon's senior officer. Glenlyon excused himself to talk to them. Then he returned, saying there were fresh orders which spoke of trouble at Glengarry. They might all have to move out sooner than he had anticipated. He bade goodnight to John and Alasdair, who set off back to their homes.

Glenlyon summoned the other officers and gave them their orders. The word went down the glen, from house to house, from officer to sergeant. It was important to maintain secrecy, they were told. No indication was to be given to the inhabitants that anything unusual was afoot. The privates themselves were to receive their instructions only at the last moment.

It must have been impossible to conceal from everyone the tension that sprang up as the messages were passed on: the sudden arrival of an officer; the silence falling in mid-conversation; the grimness in a man's face as he returned from a briefing. Certainly the stories told later about the events of that evening are of warnings, either intentional or inadvertent, given by soldiers who caught the drift of what was to happen. There is the tale of the Argyll man, leaning on a boulder and saying pointedly: 'Great stone of the glen. Great is your right to be here. Yet if you but knew what would happen this night, you would be up and away.' Or there is the soldier patting a dog and telling it, 'Grey dog, if I were you, I would be sleeping tonight out in the heather.' Or then again there is the Campbell piper who is said to have played a lament which any who heard would recognise as a warning.

It is hard to believe any of these stories. By the time the orders arrived it was dark and the storm was rising. It was no time for elaborate messages, or pipes wailing in the wind. What undoubtedly did happen, as the order was passed on or overheard, was that some soldiers salved consciences by alerting their hosts.

In the early hours of the morning the soldiers were roused and ordered to report outside. The guards had been doubled at three townships, Carnoch, Inverrigan and Achnacon, and the noise and stifled orders of one of these groups woke John MacDonald, the Chief's elder son. He dressed and walked through the snow flurries to Inverrigan, where he found Glenlyon's men preparing arms.

He demanded to know the reason for this sudden activity in the middle of the night. Glenlyon cheerfully assured him that there was no cause for alarm. Their orders were to leave immediately for Glengarry, and they faced a cold march by dawn up the Great

Above: The Devil's Staircase, by which Hamilton and his men arrived late on the morning of 13th February

Glen. As John MacDonald still hesitated, Glenlyon switched tack. Surely John could not believe they intended Glencoe some harm, he asked? Why, if that were so, would he not have warned Alasdair Og and his wife, who were after all his kith and kin?

It was the one reassurance John was able to accept. He returned to his house and went to bed, though he was unable to sleep.

At five o'clock precisely that Saturday morning Lieutenant Lindsay, with a party of soldiers behind him, rapped on the door of MacIain's house and called out to him. Lindsay's voice was friendly. They had come, he said, to bid the Chief farewell and to thank him for his hospitaliy. MacIain's wife dressed quickly, and MacIain himself began to pull on his trews, calling for a dram of whisky to be brought for the officers to see them on their way.

As he did do, Lindsay and his men burst in and shot him several times. MacIain was killed almost instantly, with one bullet through the head, another in his back. He was still only half-dressed.

A kind of frenzy seems to have struck the soldiers under Lindsay's command. They seized MacIain's wife and stripped her naked, then began to tug at the rings on her fingers. When these would not pull free they used their teeth to force them off. Wounded and badly bruised, she was released to escape into the hills. Two others in the house, probably MacIain's servants, were killed, and a third man seriously wounded. His name was Duncan Don, a messenger who occasionally brought letters for MacIain, and whose misfortune it was to be in Glencoe that night. He was left by the soldiers for dead.

MacIain's body was dragged outside the front door, where it lay with the two other corpses in the snow. There it was seen by one Archibald MacDonald, the first to confirm to his fellow clansmen that their chief was dead.

The musket fire, half-muffled by the storm, roused one of John

MacDonald's servants, who warned his master. John opened the door and saw 20 soldiers marching towards the house with bayonets fixed. He quickly woke his family and household and they all fled by the back door, escaping up the hill, west towards Meall Mór. As they climbed they met John's brother Alasdair and his wife. They had been woken by a servant, who had heard shots coming from the direction of John's house and had shaken Alasdair awake, shouting: 'It's no time for you to be sleeping when they are killing your brother at the door'. They too fled to Meall Mór.

From the hill they heard shooting from the direction of Inverrigan and Achnacon, and soon began to see flames flaring through the grey swirl of snow against the darkness.

At Inverrigan Glenlyon began his task with grim efficiency. He had ordered his men to seize the nine members of the household, including his host, MacDonald of Inverrigan, and bind them. They were then taken outside and shot one by one. A soldier, searching Inverrigan's pockets, came across a piece of paper which he brought to Glenlyon. It was Colonel Hill's letter of protection.

It may have been this which caused Glenlyon to pause in the middle of the slaughter, and order his men to hold back just as they were getting ready to shoot a young man of about 20. At that moment Captain Drummond strode up and demanded to know why the prisoner had not yet been executed. When Glenlyon's men still hesitated, Drummond himself shot the man dead.

Another youth, this time barely 13 years old, ran to Glenlyon and held on to his knees, begging to be saved. He would go anywhere with him if only his life were spared. Again Glenlyon hesitated, and again Drummond stepped in with a harsh order. The boy was killed where he knelt.

By this time Glenlyon himself was clearly sickened by the slaughter. But Drummond was a hard and methodical officer. His instructions were to see that no one escaped. Under his orders a

119

woman and a boy of about four or five were killed. One MacDonald
who escaped from Inverrigan saw two of his brothers killed, along
with three other men, and a woman. When he crept back later they
had all been buried. James Campbell, a private soldier of Glenlyon's company who saw much of the killing at Inverrigan,
watched as the houses were fired and a number of women fled in
panic into the hills.

At Achnacon, downstream from Inverrigan, Sergeant Barber
was in charge. Under his orders the operation was just as brutal.
He and his men surrounded the house of MacDonald of Achnacon,
where the household was awake and seated round the fire. The
soldiers burst in and opened fire, killing five and wounding four
others. Among the dead was Achnacon's brother, John
MacDonald of Achtriochtan, who also carried Hill's protection.

But Achnacon himself, who had been Barber's host, was only
wounded. Barber turned him over to see if he were still alive, and
as a last request Achnacon asked to be allowed to die out of doors.
Barber agreed, saying that since he had eaten his meat he would
do him the favour of killing him in the open air.

Achnachon was brought outside and Barber's soldiers closed in
on him, thrusting their muskets towards his face. At the last
moment, however, he hurled his plaid over the soldiers' heads and
charged through them, to escape into the darkness as their shots
rang out wildly. Inside the house three of the other wounded men
took advantage of the diversion and ran out of the back door.

The dead at Achnacon were dragged out and thrown onto a
dung-heap. There was more killing in the other houses nearby.
Among the dead was a small child. No one knew how he died; only
his hand was found, lying on the snow. An old man was also killed,
despite the order that only those 'under seventy' were to be shot.

At another township further down the glen a clansman called
Ronald MacDonald managed to hide just as a small group of
soldiers approached the house where his father was. They dragged
the old man from his bed, then clubbed him to the ground at the
front door. He managed to drag himself to the shelter of a nearby
house, but the soldiers, who were now setting fire to all the
cottages in the township, burnt it to the ground, and the wounded
man died inside. Ronald MacDonald came back afterwards to
collect his father's bones and bury them.

At what point in the slaughter Major Duncanson arrived with
his men is not certain. But he was far later than the five o'clock or
even 'very shortly after it' that he had promised. By the time he
rode down the smoke-filled glen a grey dawn was breaking. Glenlyon's soldiers were driving great herds of cattle, horses and sheep
down the track from the townships.

Duncanson had, however, fulfilled his task of guarding the shore
road and the mouth of the glen, which is more than Hamilton had
been able to achieve. His role had been to complete the pincer
movement from the east by bringing his men over the Devil's
Staircase and into Glencoe under the Buachaille Etive Mór. But
the weather had worsened, and the 20-mile march from Fort William was made in darkness through a driving blizzard.

At Kinlochleven the soldiers had sheltered, and Hamilton had

split them into different sections under three officers, including Major Forbes of Colonel Hill's company, who had sent the King's orders north from Edinburgh and now found himself with the duty of fulfilling them. Hamilton had instructed them to take no prisoners and to kill any man they encountered on the way. But by the time they had struggled over the high passes of the Devil's Staircase and down the track at Altnafeadh, it was eleven o'clock in the morning. They found one old man of 80 and killed him. But they had failed to stop up the escape routes to the south and west.

Hamilton and Duncanson met in the centre of the glen to take stock. They cannot have been pleased. The 'old fox' had been killed, but his two cubs had escaped along with most of their clan. When the corpses were counted, the total of those killed in the glen numbered just 38. This was less than a tenth of those they had been ordered to 'root out'. There were 900 cows and 200 horses, as well as sheep and goats to drive off. But that was not why the soldiers had been sent to Glencoe.

The MacDonalds had been helped in their flight by the storm. They had hidden on the mountain slopes, then gathered in groups and made their way out through the southern passes. There were two escape routes, neither properly secured by Glenlyon or by Hamilton. One led out towards Appin country, where friendly Stewarts could be relied on for shelter. This was up Gleann Muidhe, where MacIain had had his summer farm. It led, over rising but not impassable country, then forked south-west to Glen Creran or west to Glen Duror in the heart of Stewart country. Inevitably, in the harsh conditions of a dark February night, many of the weaker ones, including some children and older folk, died of exposure on these hills. Among them was MacIain's wife, already wounded, who survived long enough to meet up with her sons and tell them of the murder of their father.

But most of the clan managed to reach safety. Stair's odd theory that the Highlander could not survive for long in harsh weather was disproved.

The other escape route was south to Dalness, where Alasdair MacDonald of Dalness, a Glencoe kinsman, lived. He had been left out of the massacre plan, perhaps because he was a tenant under the protection of Campbell of Inverawe. This route could have been through the steep Lairig Eilde (the Pass of the Hind), but since Hamilton had failed to arrive in time to stop up the Rannoch end of the glen, the people of Achtriochtan or any of the other townships to the east could well have poured out through the Lairig Gartain, or even, skirting the Buachaille Etive Mór, down Glen Etive. They must have been amazed and relieved to see no sign of a redcoat.

There were other reasons, besides the storm, which helped the escapers, and here the sworn testimony of witnesses gives way to legends which may contain a kernel of truth.

Many of the soldiers who had been stationed in Glencoe were Highlanders. True, they were Campbells or Argyll men, but they would still have found their native laws of hospitality hard to break so bloodily. Many of them undoubtedly allowed Mac-

Donalds to escape or pretended to kill to deceive their officers. There is the story, repeated in endless variations, of the woman and her baby who hide in the hills as the soldiers search. The crying of the baby gives them away and a soldier is despatched to kill them. When he comes on them he finds a dog which has followed on their heels; he kills it instead and returns to show, by the blood on his sword, that the deed has been done.

Or there is the story of the soldier sent to bayonet a woman to death who hears her crooning a lullaby to her baby: it is the same song he used to hear as a child and he is so moved that he spares them. The song has even been given this haunting Gaelic verse:

Cold, cold this night is my bed
Cold, cold this night is my child.
Lasting, lasting this night my sleep.
I in my shroud and thou in my arm.
The shadow of death creeps over me.
The warm pulse of my love will not stir
The wind of the heights thy sleep-lulling.
The close-clinging snow of the peaks thy mantle.

That there were heroes and poets among those who died or escaped is also part of the legend. Ranald of the Shield, a great MacDonald warrior and a bard, who fought at the battle of Inverlochy in 1645 and won a famous duel at the battle of Worcester, is said to have been killed at Glencoe. The great Gaelic poet Murdoch Matheson is also supposed to have escaped and composed the most famous of the laments for those who died:

Dear to me are the white bodies of those who were generous, manly delightful men. Alas, that one should see our nobles defenceless at the mercy of those who hate them; yet had we been under arms before the hunt gathered against the land; there were redcoats there who would never have returned to the king's army.
No doctor could have healed your gaping wounds: the ample rewarders of poets were bleeding under their shirts. But, given equal odds between you and the Lowland band, the rough feathered birds of the mountains would have screamed, befouled from your enemies corpses . . . King of the angels, creator of the elements, take care of the souls of those who have passed over. Your numbers have been thinned in the rough awakening of that exchange.

By the afternoon of Saturday 13th, Glencoe was silent. Smoke drifted from the smouldering thatch, and ravens and buzzards had begun to wheel overhead. Some of the bolder members of the clan crept back to search for bodies or survivors, but the proper burial of the twelfth Chief of Clan Iain Abrach, on Eilean Munde, would wait for many days longer. Most of those who had escaped were by now safely in Dalness or Appin, and no one could be certain that the soldiers would not return to finish the job. That night the wind rose again and brought gusts of snow to cover the burnt timbers and the stains of deep red.

Overleaf: 'Wreaths of snow, in a vehement storm . . . wherein the greater part of them perished . . .'
Snowclouds over Loch Achtriochtan

9

'AGAINST THE LAWS OF NATURE'

ON 14th February, the day after the massacre, Colonel Hill sat in the Governor's room at Fort William to write a report on the Highlands to the Marquis of Tweeddale, Lord Chancellor of Scotland. Matters, he said, were proceeding well: Glengarry had finally surrendered his castle; a successful expedition had been mounted in the Western Isles; and . . . 'I have also ruined Glencoe. Old Glencoe and Achtriochtan being killed with 36 more, the rest by reason of an extraordinary storm escaped, but their goods are a prey and their houses to the fire . . . I hope this example of justice and severity upon Glencoe will be enough.'

Enough for what? Hill does not elaborate. His letter is the brief and non-committal report of a military man. Remorse, regret, if he felt any, is not allowed to show.

Breadalbane, on the other hand, heard the news with mounting panic. He was in London, where he had stayed all winter, receiving regular news from the Highlands from his cousin, Colin Campbell of Carwhin, a lawyer who acted as his agent in Scotland. His first response to Carwhin's description of what had happened was to express astonishment, to claim he knew nothing of the plan, and to attempt to shift blame. 'I have expostulated about the unreasonable and mad measures taken in it, and that E.A.'s [Earl of Argyll's] men be the executioners, and that after they had taken the oath. I fear innocent persons be the sufferers in the same measure. When I told E.A. he said he hopt the king would protect them. I said it was a far cry to Lochawe . . .' In Campbell language 'a far cry to Lochawe' meant that what happened in the Highlands bore little relation to the way things were seen in the south. Breadalbane knew that if he were associated with the affair his standing in Scotland might be destroyed. 'O! how it will reflect', he added, 'and needed not if wisely managed. I am exceedingly concerned about it.'

By early March Carwhin had told Breadalbane that his name was being connected with the massacre. Breadalbane blamed his cousin Glenlyon. 'It's villainy to accuse me for Glenlyon's madness . . .', he wrote. And later: 'Ane ill and miraculous fate follows unfortunate Glenlyon in the whole tract of his life. He is not to be mended. I hope he will go to Flanders.'

Argyll took malicious pleasure in Breadalbane's discomfiture, and told him that the latest rumour was that his clansmen had been buying Glencoe cows 'for a dollar the piece'. Breadalbane responded angrily by saying that if that were true he would 'make them restore them to the widows and fatherless'. But he sensed that he was being deliberately isolated. Both Argyll and Stair, he wrote, were leaving with the King for Flanders, and Argyll was 'a very pleased man'.

He knew, perhaps more than they did, that Glencoe could prove dangerous eventually for anyone connected with it. He sent instructions to Campbell of Barcaldine, his steward, to make contact with those Glencoe MacDonalds who had escaped to Appin. A messenger was duly despatched to the west coast, and when he had found MacIain's sons, John and Alasdair, he made them an offer: if they would sign a document saying that the Earl of Breadalbane was innocent of the massacre, then he would use

Above: Twin sentinels on
the southern flank of
Glencoe – the Aonach
Dubh and the Geàrr Aonach

Opposite: Flooded bog-land
in the shadow of Buchaille
Etive Beag

his influence to procure a pardon for their people, and have them
restored to their lands. It is not known what response the
messenger received. But it can be guessed at, and it brought no
consolation to a by-now-distraught Breadalbane. 'I am as free of
accession as the man of Spain', he insisted to Carwhin, '. . . I
neither know Colonel Hill's orders first or last about Glencoe.'

There was no such hand-wringing from the army. Shortly after
the massacre, Hamilton wrote to Livingstone, now back in Edinburgh, saying that he had managed to round up some fugitives. On
26th February Livingstone replied, saying he had given instructions that there were to be no prisoners. 'The taking of them is but
a burden to the government . . .', he wrote, 'let no prisoners be
brought in, but let them be dispatched in the place where they are
found, for such robbers and thieves are not to be treated as regular
enemies.'

Reports from both Hamilton and Hill went to Stair in London,
and on 5th March Stair sent a testy reply to Hill:

'There is much talk of it here, that they are murdered in their
beds after they had taken the allegiance; for the last I know
nothing of it. I am sure neither you nor anybody impowered to
treat or give indemnity did give him the oath, and to take it from
anybody else after the diet elapsed, did import nothing. All I
regrate is, that any of the sept got away, and there is necessity to
prosecute them to the utmost.'

Perhaps there is a hint here of Stair too beginning to seek

excuses, but he was more irritated than anxious. The King had left for Flanders and he was preparing to follow him. Glencoe was yesterday's business.

By now, however, the rumours in Scotland had begun to grow. At first they were wild: stories of a clan battle between Campbells and MacDonalds; hints of an army ambush in which MacIain had died, sword in hand. But by the end of March the story was more explicit. It was helped by the arrival in Edinburgh of Argyll's regiment *en route* for Flanders. Glenlyon's soldiers now gave their own accounts, with reluctance or defiance according to their temperaments. Glenlyon himself attempted to carry it off with bravado. In the Royal Coffee House in Parliament Close, he boasted about the action and announced he would do it again if necessary. 'I would stab any man in Scotland or England without asking the cause, if the King gave me orders', he announced, 'and it is every good subject's duty so to do.' He and his men, he said, would apply to the Privy Council for a reward for good service.

Glenlyon made it clear that he had only been carrying out orders. Others did the same. Copies of both Hamilton's and Duncanson's orders began to circulate in Jacobite hands, and they could only have been given out if they had been released by the officers who had received them.

The rumours reached Fort William as well, and Colonel Hill sensed that a scapegoat was being sought. He had already written to the Earl of Portland, one of William's closest advisers, suggesting that it might be sensible to allow the Glencoe men to return home in peace. Now he felt the need to defend himself to Tweeddale:

'I understand that there are some severe reflections upon the action in Glenco, and that perhaps by good men too. Therefore I think it my duty to give your Lordship a more particular account thereof.'

Hill went on to blame MacIain for being late in taking the oath. He claimed that, instead of going straight to Inveraray, MacIain had spent some time with Alasdair MacDonald of Glengarry, and had written to the Sheriff at Inveraray rather than going in person. There is no evidence for this, and it is an unaccountable aberration on Hill's part. But he was plainly worried that the affair might rebound on him; he was old, on the point of retirement; and he was still owed money by the Government, which he would never receive if he were now to be blamed for a massacre. He wrote worriedly to Tweeddale:

'I had several orders from the Commander in Chief and all extraordinary strict to destroy these people and take no prisoners, and (lest I prove remiss) another of the same orders was directed to my Lieutenant-Colonel to do the same, and after all that another order under the King's hand to root out that sept of thieves . . . If any censure the severity of man's justice, yet the Justice of God is to reverenced, for there was much blood on these people's hands . . .'

Tweeddale heard too from an ambitious young politician called James Johnston of Wariston, who would soon become joint Secretary of State for Scotland with Stair himself. 'This business of Glencoe makes a scurvy noise,' wrote Johnston. 'Major Duncanson's Christian order is in the coffee-houses. It's said that Glencoe had been admitted to take the oath and that the troops were quartered upon them and so against all the laws of hospitality and in cold blood killed their hosts, that women and children were not spared.'

On 12th April the gossip reached printed form in the *Paris Gazette*, which carried a brief account of the affair. It announced that 'the Laird of Glencoe was butchered several days ago in the most barbarous manner', and it put the blame specifically on Glenlyon and on Hill.

But by now the insatiable Charles Leslie, in London, had also heard of the affair and had sent north for more detailed information. On 20th April he published the first complete account of the massacre in pamphlet form, disguising his sources (and himself) by titling it 'Letter from a Gentleman in Edinburgh to his Friend in London after the Massacre'. It was 4,000 words long, and remarkably accurate. Very little of his detailed report was later to be challenged, and the fact that he included *verbatim* both Hamilton and Duncanson's orders, the latter with its damning phrase, 'this is by the King's special command', meant that the affair could no longer be ignored.

Leslie drew as much pathos as he could from the events in Glencoe that February day:

'How dismal may you imagine the case of the poor women and children was then! It was lamentable past expression, their husbands and fathers and near relations were forced to flee for their lives; they themselves almost stript, and nothing left them, and their houses being burnt, and not one house nearer than six miles; and to get thither they were to pass over mountains, wreaths of snow, in a vehement storm, wherein the greatest part of them perished through hunger and cold. It fills me with horror to think of poor stript children and women, some with child, and some giving suck, wrestling against a storm in the mountains and heaps of snow, and at length overcome, and give over, and fall down, and die miserably.'

But with the instincts of a journalist Leslie went on to direct his readers towards those with whom the ultimate responsibility lay:

'As to the Government, I will not meddle with it; or whether these officers who murdered Glencoe had such orders as they pretended from the Government, the Government knows that best, and how to vindicate their honour, and punish the murderers who pretended their authority and still stand upon it. But as to the fact of Glencoe, you may depend upon it as certain and undeniable.'

For the time being, however, the principals had gone to ground. Breadalbane had left London on 12th April, the day the *Paris Gazette* appeared, and had retreated to his estates. 'It was', as he himself liked saying, 'a far cry to Loch Awe'.

Stair, at camp with William in Flanders, dismissed the outcry briefly in a letter to Hill: 'It's true that affair of Glencoe was very ill-executed, but 'tis strange to me that means so much regret for a sept of thieves.'

Overleaf: Glencoe looking east from the valley where MacIain's summer house stood

William himself was too preoccupied to give the matter more than passing consideration. But his attitude was undoubtedly reflected in a further letter Stair sent back to Hill: 'When you do your duty in a thing so necessary to rid the country of thieving, you need not trouble yourself to take the pains to vindicate yourself . . . when you do right, you need fear nobody.'

For one participant, however, the strain was beginning to tell. The remorse that Glenlyon had first felt that dark morning in Glencoe, when he tried to put a halt to the shooting, had returned to haunt him. On 30th June Leslie travelled out to Brentford in Middlesex, where Argyll's regiment was quartered before leaving for Flanders. There he verified the story at first-hand and saw both Captain Drummond and Glenlyon. One soldier to whom he spoke said that Glenlyon's guilt was almost visible. 'Glencoe hangs about Glenlyon night and day. You may see him in his face.'

In the hills of Lochaber, the refugees from Glencoe were still outlaws. They were harboured and fed by Stewarts of Appin, and helped by Keppoch Macdonalds and Camerons of Lochiel. History records one notable gesture of friendship when Archibald Mac-Donald, a laird from the Western Hebrides, whose links with the MacIains stretched back 300 years, sailed a boat laden with meal from North Uist southwards, then up Loch Linnhe, to deposit it on the shores of Loch Leven for the starving Glencoe people.

For months the Government continued to withold its pardon. From Fort William Hill had continued to urge the Privy Council to permit the survivors to return to their home and to swear a new oath of loyalty. But it was not until August that he was allowed to issue a proclamation that he 'received the men of Glencoe unto his Majesty's protection, upon their submission to his Majesty's mercy, taking the oath of allegiance, and giving security to live peaceably, and answer, as law will, in all time coming for any crimes shall hereafter be committed by them . . .'

Only then could John MacDonald, now thirteenth chief of Glencoe, swear the oath his father had once taken in Inveraray, and bring his people home. He went in all humility, promising Hill 'to live under His Majesty's royal protection in such a manner that the Government shall not repent or give you cause to blush for the favour you have done me and my people'.

Hill placed the clan under the superiority of Argyll, but the Campbell yoke was now less important than the simple business of survival. 'The Glenco men are abundantly civil,' Hill was able to report to his friend Duncan Forbes, the Laird of Culloden. 'They are now my Lord Argyle's men; for 'twas very necessary they should be under some person of power, and of honesty to the Government.' Slowly the houses in Glencoe were rebuilt, a few head of cattle brought in, the glen nursed back to life again.

In London the affair was firmly in the political arena, and there was no lack of parties interested in using it to their own advantage. Johnston of Wariston, now joint Secretary of State with Stair, and determined to take over the full office, favoured an enquiry into this 'foul business'. But he was clever enough to assure everyone that the purpose of his campaign was not personal ambition but a simple desire to clear the King's name.

William himself had been through the worst summer of his campaign. The terrible defeat at Steinkirk, where thousands of his soldiers died, including General Hugh Mackay, was a cause for despair. That winter again he had little time for Scotland, but even he could not ignore the outcry. Queen Mary, who was horrified when she heard of the slaughter, added her voice to the demands for justice.

In the spring of 1693 William at last agreed to appoint the Duke of Hamilton a Commissioner to the Scots Parliament, with orders to hold an enquiry into the massacre.

Livingstone wrote to Hamilton to tell him the news. He affected the weariness of a soldier complaining of the interference of politicians, but Hamilton may have sensed in Livingstone's letter the tone of a man beginning to affect a deliberate vagueness:

'Since my last, it is resolved that your Colonel must come in person to Edinburgh, and give an account of the Glenco business. It is not that anybody thinks that thieving tribe did not deserve to be destroyed, but that it should have been done by such as was quartered amongst them, makes a great noise. I suppose I may have pressed it somewhat upon your Colonel, knowing how slow he was in the exaction of such things . . . I should be glad you would let me have all the circumstances you know of that matter etc. Sir, your humble servant, T. Livingstoun.'

But it was not until 1695 – two years later – that Hill and other witnesses central to the affair were finally summoned to appear before a Commission of Enquiry set up 'under the Broad Seal' and headed by the Marquis of Tweeddale and the Earl of Annandale. The Commission's other members were Lord Murray, Sir James Stuart, Adam Cockburn of Ormiston, Sir Archibald Hope of Rankeillor, Sir William Hamilton of Whitelaw, Sir James Ogilvie and Adam Drummond of Megginch. They were part of Scotland's legal establishment, but their loyalties were not necessarily wholeheartedly with the King. One or two had been King James's men in their time and might still nurse secret Jacobite sentiments. As a body they were eager to show that the Scots Parliament, to whom they would report, still had an independent voice. But their own independence was strictly limited. They had been appointed by 'His Majesty', and in the end they were answerable to him.

They set about their task efficiently enough, however, calling as witnesses Hill and his officers, Livingstone, Hamilton, Campbell of Ardkinglas, the lawyers who had considered MacIain's oath in Edinburgh, and those who had scored it from the register. They called ten men who had been in or near Glencoe on the day of the massacre, including John MacDonald, the thirteenth chief, his brother Alasdair, and Alexander MacDonald, son of the murdered tacksman of Achtriochtan. All were sent a special letter of protection to ensure their presence in the great hall at Holyroodhouse during the last week of May and the first three weeks of June 1695. The arrival of these men, survivors from a distant and now notorious place, caused a sensation on the streets of Edinburgh.

But only one of the soldiers who had been in Glencoe that day, James Campbell, a private in Glenlyon's company, who had not gone to Flanders, appeared before the Commission.

Hamilton did not obey the summons to attend. And those who were in Flanders – Glenlyon, Drummond, Duncanson, Lindsay, Lundie, Sergeant Barber and the others – were not asked by the Commissioners to attend, perhaps for fear of offending the King by summoning his soldiers from the battlefield.

The Commission set itself four tasks: to find out what had led up to the massacre; what had happened on the day itself; who had given the orders; and lastly to reach a conclusion – 'the Commissioners' humble opinion of the true state and acccount of the whole business'.

The first of these produced a dramatic piece of evidence. Breadalbane's Private Articles at Achallader, the secret undertakings he was said to have proposed to the chiefs to secure their support, were read out in public for the first time. To the Commissioners the deal smelt of high treason, and warrants went out for Breadalbane's arrest. He was seized and thrown into prison at Edinburgh Castle, where he feared for his life. His son set off immediately for Flanders to plead for him, though this was more easily said than done. It took four months for William to grant him an audience.

Witness after witness gave evidence, their depositions written out, signed and sworn, and by 24th June the Commissioners were ready to draw up their report and send it for consideration by the Scots Parliament.

Their conclusions were carefully drafted. They judged it wrong that MacIain's oath should have been obliterated and they be-

lieved that Stair *had* been aware that it had been sworn, despite having claimed in his letters that he had been ignorant of the fact. The next part was the hardest. 'There was nothing in the King's instructions', said the Report, 'to warrant the committing of the foresaid slaughter, even as to the thing itself, and far less as to the manner of it.'

Their reasoning was tortuous. The King, they argued, had ordered nothing concerning Glencoe save that 'if [they] could be well separated from the rest, it would be a proper vindication of the public justice to exirpate that sept of thieves.' This, the Commissioners suggested, 'plainly intimates, that it was in his Majesty's mind that they could not be separated from the rest of these rebels, unless they refused his mercy by continuing in arms and refusing the allegiance, and that, even in that case, they were only to be proceeded against in the way of public justice, and no other way.'

These were weasel words. But the Commissioners knew that their own survival in office depended on exonerating the King, and they were content to fix the blame instead on his chief minister in Scotland. When it came to considering Stair's role they did not equivocate, and even the critical Charles Leslie, as he read their report, cannot have had cause to complain:

'Secretary Stair's letters . . . were no ways warranted, but quite exceeded the King's foresaid instructions; since the said letters, without any insinuation of any method to be taken that might well separate the Glenco men from the rest, did, in place of prescribing a vindication of publick justice, order them to be cut off and rooted out in earnest, and to purpose, and that suddenly, and secretly, and quietly, and all on a sudden, which are the express terms of the said letters; and comparing them, and the other letters, with what ensued, appear to have been the only warrant and cause of their slaughter, which in effect, was a barbarous murder . . .'

The Report was sent to Flanders, and on 26th June the Scots Parliament met to debate it. Seldom had its members witnessed scenes of such excitement. They were, after all, engaged on a process of impeachment against the King's own representative, and in so doing asserting a measure of independence which went far beyond what most of them had ever contemplated.

Support for Stair, which had never been exactly whole-hearted, melted away. Only the Earl of Argyll ventured to speak on his behalf and he was ruled out of order. The debate on Glencoe went on into July, and in the middle of it Stair produced a defence. Drawn up by his brother Hew, it complained that he had been 'mightily prejudged' by the Commissioners' report; his letters had been taken out of context, and he had not been allowed to comment on them. The Glencoe men, he said, 'were very ill men, rebels, papists, robbers and thieves, which did not justify any inhumanity in their execution, but did expose them more to legal severity than other subjects'.

He too quoted the King's orders, but only to demonstrate that they had been too brutally interpreted by Livingstone, Glenlyon and by those who had decided to violate the laws of hospitality.

'Though the command of superior officers be very absolute, yet no command against the laws of nature is binding,' he pointed out, 'so that a soldier, retaining his commission, ought to refuse to execute any barbarity . . .'

It was a lengthy defence, containing minute analysis of every letter quoted, but it was rejected out of hand by Parliament, which was outraged that its deliberations should be challenged while it was still in session. Hew Dalrymple was censured for his interference. But just in case it should be thought that Stair's excuses had any merit, the Lord Advocate's office prepared an equally lengthy rebuttal.

Finally, after a lengthy sitting, a vote was taken on the question of whether Stair had exceeded the King's warrant. The motion was carried by a large majority.

On 10th July 1695 an 'Address by Parliament to the King, Touching the Murder of the Glencoe Men' was drawn up and sent to William. It was a brisk and straightforward document. It accepted as a premise that the King was innocent, but it went on to describe the massacre in the following terms: 'the killing of the Glencoe men being on that occasion unwarrantable, as well as the manner of doing it being barbarous and inhumane, we proceeded to vote the killing of them a murder'. Stair was found guilty of being 'the original cause of this unhappy business'. He stood condemned for the way in which he had ordered the destruction of Glencoe 'with a great deal of zeal as a thing acceptable and of publick use'. How he should be dealt with was left to the King to decide 'as you in your royal wisdom shall think fit'.

Breadalbane, still languishing in the Castle, was not mentioned, and with him Argyll slipped conveniently from the record.

Livingstone was cleared, because he was 'ignorant of the peculiar circumstances of the Glenco men', and because he might have thought Stair's instruction came directly from the King.

Hill was found to be 'clear and free of the slaughter of the Glenco men'. He had not urged it; he had held back until the last minute; and he had then given only a general order to Hamilton to obey his superior officer. Hamilton, on the other hand, was judged worthy of prosecution. He had failed to answer a summons to testify and there was *prima facie* evidence against him. 'We agreed that, from what appeared, he was not clear of the murder of the Glencoe men.'

Glenlyon, Drummond, Lindsay, Lundie and Barber were all judged to be guilty of a 'slaughter under trust', and Parliament recommended they should stand trial. 'Considering that the actors have barbarously killed men under trust, we humbly desire your Majesty would be pleased to send the actors home and give orders to your Advocate to prosecute them according to law.'

Finally Parliament suggested that the King might extend some charity towards the victims. Those who had escaped the slaughter were 'reduced to great poverty' and had pleaded for some form of compensation in a document which spoke, with slight exaggeration, of 500 horses and 1500 cows.

There was, however, to be no reparation. There was also to be no question of the King sending back any of his officers or men from

Overleaf: The north flank of Aonach Dubh on left, looking west along Glencoe

Flanders. William was irritated by the persistence of his Parliament in Edinburgh, and, though it had cleared him, he wanted nothing to do with the affair. The summer of 1695 was turning out to be another bad campaigning season, and the Queen was no longer there to prompt his conscience on Highland matters – Mary had died the previous year.

But some things had changed. The ground was slipping imperceptibly away from Stair, who no longer automatically had the ear of the King, and who was eventually obliged to resign the Secretaryship and return to his estates. His father died that year, and he succeeded to the title of viscount, but his influence was less than it had ever been.

Finally, in October, the King came back to London. Pressed by Breadalbane's son, he agreed to release the Earl from Edinburgh castle. It is clear from the wording of William's command that he did so out of pique with his Parliament in Scotland, who had prosecuted a man for carrying out negotiations 'for which he had our exoneration and approbation'. At any rate Breadalbane was now free, and he returned thankfully to his own estates.

It was another two months before William could bring himself to consider the matter further. Then, on 2nd December, he summoned those members of the Scots Privy Council who were in London to come to Kensington Palace. He informed them that he was concerned about the Glencoe affair but had known little of it at the time. He wished to hear from those present, and he waited as Stair argued in his defence and Johnston of Wariston, his rival, replied. They were then dismissed.

After that – silence. William gave no indication of his views, but his lack of action indicates quite clearly where he stood. There was no order to Glenlyon or the others to return from Flanders to stand trial. And Stair was pardoned. A 'scroll of discharge' was issued from the Palace.

'His Majesty being well satisfied that the said John Viscount of Stair, hath rendered him many faithful services, and being well assured of his affection and good intentions, and being graciously pleased to pardon, cover, and secure him now after the demission of his office . . . and particularly, his Majesty considering that the manner of execution of the men of Glenco was contrary to the laws of humanity and hospitality, being done by these soldiers who for some days had been quartered amongst them and entertained by them, which was a fault in the actors, or these who gave the immediate orders on the place; but the said Viscount of Stair, then Secretary of State, being at London, many hundred miles distant, he could have no knowledge of, nor accession to, the method of that execution . . . he had no hand in the barbarous manner of execution.'

Parliament had done what it could, and in one sense what it had achieved was remarkable – one of the last truly independent gestures it was to make before its final extinction in the Act of Union. It had secured the resignation of the King's minister, the imprisonment of one of his most powerful feudal barons, and had heard the evidence showing that murder had been committed.

But it had also demonstrated its impotence. There had been no examination of the role of Argyll, who had given counsel and encouragement to Stair during the days in December 1691 and January 1692 when the plan took shape, and whose regiment was used to carry out the action. There had been no proper scrutiny of Breadalbane's role, no curtain raised to explore the generations of hostility that lay behind his quarrel with MacIain that day at Achallader, or to inquire whether it was he who finally pointed the finger at Glencoe and quietly explained to Stair how the passes could be secured and secrecy and suddenness assured.

The King was exonerated, as he had to be, despite his signature at the top and bottom of an order as unequivocal as any ever issued by a reigning monarch. He took the easy way out by blaming those lower down the hierarchy, but he still failed to send them back for trial, and Parliament was forced to accept his indifference meekly. Those who later sought to defend the King by suggesting that he had simply failed to read the order, have little to sustain their case; nowhere is there any evidence that William, either before or afterwards, disapproved of the objective embodied in the plan: that a small tribe of his own people should simply be eliminated.

It was left to Charles Leslie to pin the blame firmly where he judged it to lie, and if he was over-passionate in doing so he may have been frustrated to find, as many a journalist has done since, that exposing a guilty man does not automatically bring him to book. Leslie reprinted his original report, together with the Commission's findings, and added his own derisive commentary, publishing the whole as a pamphlet under the title, 'Gallienus Redivivus, or MURDER WILL OUT, ETC., Being a True Account of the DE-WITTING of GLENCO'.

The references were straightforward: Gallienus was the Roman tyrant who ordered his men to kill all those who criticised him; the De Witt brothers were two of William's enemies in Holland who had been eliminated with his knowledge and consent.

'Here is a precedent made, and that by Parliament, that the King may send his guards and cut any man's throat in the nation in cold blood . . . What can you expect from him but to be Glencoed for your pains? He scorned to excerpt the pitiful women, as Gallienus did. What need they be excerpted? Why, he excerpted nobody!'

Leslie concluded with a hope which was to become something of a Jacobite slogan: 'Qui Glencoat Glencoabitur' – 'He who Glencoes, will himself be Glencoed'.

The prediction was not to be fulfilled. William died in March 1702 after his horse had stumbled on a molehill, and the Jacobites toasted the 'little gentleman in black velvet' who had been responsible for his death.

Stair lived quietly on his estates for several years, but returned under Queen Anne to work for the Union of the Scottish and English Parliaments, which had always been his great goal. In 1703 he was made first Earl of Stair, and three years later he was one of the Commissioners sent from Scotland to negotiate the Treaty of Union. The signing away of Scotland's independence won him many bitter enemies, but he never wavered from his conviction that the Union would be to the ultimate advantage of

his country. He died in his sleep on 7th January 1707 at the age of 58, while a heated debate was being pursued in Parliament over the Treaty. He was followed to the end and and beyond by the dark rumours which always surrounded the Dalrymple family: on his death it was at once suggested he had hanged himself in remorse for the massacre of Glencoe.

Opposite: The River Coe looking west towards Meall Mór

Argyll was honoured, too. William trusted him and gave him the title of duke in June 1701, two years before his death at the age of 50. In the public mind, however, he was more noted for a fondness for women – 'a foible', as his biographer noted, 'that is frequently met with in the greatest men, and from which few of his family were free'.

Breadalbane, however, lived on, and in his old age he became a Highland chief again. Whether he had been soured by his experiences in prison, or whether he had always at heart been a Jacobite, he refused to vote for the Union in 1707, and in 1715 he supported the rising under the Old Pretender by sending 400 of his men to fight at the battle of Sheriffmuir. Even the Gaelic bards praised his action, and it was a Keppoch MacDonald who wrote a poem celebrating the 'gold-spangled banner' of Breadalbane. He himself was too old to be there, but after the suppression of the rebellion, government troops were sent to Balloch Castle to arrest him. The story is told that when the arresting officer went into his bedroom, Breadalbane was lying semi-conscious on his bed. The officer touched him on the shoulder and said: 'Sir, you are my prisoner.' Breadalbane looked at him scornfully and replied: 'Your prisoner! I am the prisoner of God Almighty and 81 years of age.' Turning to an attendant he ordered: 'Duncan, take that poor man away, and get him out of the country before my people get to hear of the insult he has offered me.' The Earl was left in peace, and died a year later, in March 1717.

Robert Campbell of Glenlyon never returned to Scotland from Flanders. He died at Bruges in August 1696, still overwhelmed by debts. But his son, John Campbell, led Breadalbane's men into battle at Sheriffmuir, where they fought alongside the MacDonalds. It is said that when Glengarry raised the subject of Glencoe with him, he answered: 'Of that I am sackless, the only rivalry I shall have with a MacDonald is, which of us will wreak upon yon ranks the injuries of our King.' The two men shook hands and took the field together. John Campbell survived the battle, went into exile, and returned to support Bonnie Prince Charlie in 1745. Pursued as a rebel, he died on his own estate after hiding out in the woods to escape the redcoat search parties. With the next generation, the direct Glenlyon line died out.

In Glencoe, the MacDonalds rebuilt their homes and picked up the threads of their old life. John MacDonald, the thirteenth chief, erected a new house at Carnoch; the foundation stone, marked 1708, is set in the burial vault of Eilean Munde. Their fighting spirit was not broken, for in 1715 Alasdair Og, MacIain's younger son, led 100 men at Sheriffmuir, and in 1745, the fourteenth chief fought with 150 followers at the Battle of Culloden. Prince Charles Edward had welcomed the new MacIain and made him a member of his Council. A famous story tells of how the Prince's army oc-

cupied Linlithgow, near the big house at Newliston which was a family residence of the Stairs. Fearful that MacIain with his fiery band of MacDonalds would wreak vengeance on the Stairs by pillaging their house, he ordered them to camp a long way off. But the Chief heard of this and insisted that he and his men should be assigned instead to guard the house so that they could prove to the world that the purity of their cause was not tainted by any 'vileinye of hate'.

The MacDonalds of Glencoe were punished, with others of their clan, for their devotion to the Stuart cause. Those who survived Culloden in 1746 returned to the glen, but government soldiers once again marched on them from Fort William, burning houses, including John MacDonald's new one at Carnoch, and driving off their cattle for the second time.

This time recovery was slower, but soon there were crofts huddled together again, mainly at the Loch Leven end of the glen, and the population had nearly doubled. By the 19th century, when men began to give way to sheep, the people had moved up towards Ballachulish, where a slate quarry provided work for some. From 1830 on there was a steady drift away from Glencoe, with many joining the spate of emigrations.

The MacIain line did not die out until recently. Indeed, it may still continue. Major Duncan MacDonald, the twentieth Chief of Glencoe, who sold his lands there in 1894, had three children. The first died unmarried; the third, a daughter, married into the English family of de Hoghton, but none of her heirs now survives. The second son, however, Roy Cameron MacDonald, became an aircraftsman in the RAF in the Second World War. He was then, following the death of his elder brother, the twenty-second Chief of Glencoe, but whether he lived through the war, or married to produce an heir, is unknown. Just possibly there is somewhere a proper claimant for one of the most romantic titles in Scotland.

The glen today is a beauty spot, visited by tourists and by mountaineers who prize the sheer face of its cliffs for the very inaccessibility which made the valley once a fortress, or a trap. A memorial to those who died there nearly 300 years ago has been built alongside the River Coe, and every year on 13th February a small band of dedicated MacDonalds gathers to hold a service in its shadows.

Nothing built by human beings, save for the burial ground at Eilean Munde, survives to remind the visitor of the events of that day. The chief's house at Carnoch has gone; the site of MacIain's summer house is a matter of dispute; the stones of the little cottages have long since sunk beneath the ground.

But at the place where the old township of Inverrigan once was, nine trees have been planted. They stand in memory of the nine MacDonalds who died there, bound and shot one by one, as Robert Campbell of Glenlyon looked on in sickened horror. To some, therefore, they may recall not just the victims, but the human frailty of those who tried, and failed, to put an end to a slaughter they knew should never have begun.

Opposite: The snow-covered face of the Aonach Eagach

Overleaf: Today the glen, unchanged, is visited by tourists, prized by mounta

147

EPILOGUE

The massacre of Glencoe still arouses strong and deeply divided feelings in Scotland. In the course of my research I was struck both by its capacity to provoke passionate argument, and by the diversity of opinion about what really happened, and why. In some ways attitudes have changed little over the years. For instance, one senior member of Clan Campbell described it, only half-jokingly, as a 'piffling incident' involving 'some 32 illiterate tinkers, cattle rustlers and general miscreants . . .' An equally senior member of Clan Donald, however, addressing the small service of commemoration which is held each year on the anniversary of the massacre, spoke of the need to keep alive the memory of what had been 'an act of brutal treachery'. In his eyes its importance lay in its capacity to remind the world how vulnerable a minority can be when it stands in the way of a powerful majority. To a Scottish Nationalist with whom I discussed it, the incident served as a forceful demonstration of English contempt for Scottish interests. And to a Marxist historian it was an example of exploitation by an expanding propertied class. All of these views contain elements of truth. But, in writing this account I have tried to keep fact and opinion as far apart as possible; to make the distinction between what actually happened and what was believed to have happened as clear as I could; and where propaganda became part of the tale to point out whose propaganda it was.

Wherever possible in quoting from letters and contemporary documents I have used the original spelling, except where it obscures the meaning of a sentence. When it comes to Gaelic words or names, I have used modern spelling.

The telling is helped by the unusual amount of contemporary documentation available. The Report of the Commission of Enquiry, which is in the Public Record Office in London, contains the official account of the massacre, based on first-hand evidence from witnesses called before it. Some caution is necessary in interpreting it – the language is not as dispassionate as perhaps it should be, and there are tantalising gaps in the evidence. But it is the most reliable version available of the event itself and the circumstances leading up to it. The letters written by Stair and others, as well as Duncanson's and Hamilton's orders, together with many other relevant documents, are collected in the Maitland Club's Papers on the period, sometimes known as the Highland Papers. I have given much credit to Charles Leslie, the Irish non-juror and pamphleteer who first published the story in detail. His report accords remarkably well with the official account, and it came out three years earlier, which is excellent journalism. Others were doubtless involved in compiling it as well as he, but Leslie deserves credit for publishing it at some risk to himself. The Register of the Privy Council of Scotland supplies much of the political background and recounts, among other things, the misdeeds of generations of MacDonalds. *The Black Book of Taymouth* is a splendid collection of documents on the

Breadalbane Campbells. Other original manuscripts are in the Scottish National Library, the Scottish Record Office, and the Edinburgh Public Library. They are listed below.

Among more modern works I would single out three that have been particularly helpful, partly for the wealth of information they contain, but also because they challenge some of the more romantic preconceptions about that absorbing and traumatic period of Scottish history: David Stevenson's *Alasdair MacColla and the Highland Problem in the 17th century*; *A Highland History* by the Earl of Cromartie; and last, but very far from least, John Prebble's *Glencoe*, because it has both inspired and provoked me, and because, as I proceeded, I found very few by-ways which did not already bear the Prebble footprint.

For permission to reproduce pictures in their possession, I am indebted to the National Portrait Gallery in London for the portraits of James II, Mary II and William III; to the Scottish National Portrait Gallery for the portraits of Robert Campbell of Glenlyon and the first Earl of Breadalbane; to the Earl of Stair for the portrait of the the first Earl; and to His Grace the Duke of Argyll and the Pilgrim Press for the portrait of the first Duke. The family trees of the senior descent of the Campbells, of the Lords of the Isles, and of the Glenorchy Campbells are by kind permission, respectively, of His Grace the Duke of Argyll, the Clan Donald Centre, Skye (photographed by Skye Photographic), and the Scottish National Portrait Gallery. The photograph by Jim Nicholson of Duncanson's despatch was kindly made available by the National Trust of Scotland. The photographs of arms and household goods in common use during the 17th century were provided by the Highland Folk Museum and the National Museum of Antiquities of Scotland. I am particularly grateful to Gerald Corbett for making a special journey to Stranraer and Edinburgh to photograph three of these portraits, and to David Worth for his graphic skill in producing the maps on pages 22, 23 and 91.

151

BIBLIOGRAPHY

Acts of the Parliament of Scotland (Edinburgh 1814–1875)

Balfour-Melville, E W M, *An Account of the Proceedings of the Estates in Scotland 1689–1690* (1954)

Bannatyne Club, *Leven and Melville Papers* (1843)

Browne, James, *A History of the Highlands and the Highland Clans* (1850)

Buchan, John *The Massacre of Glencoe* (1933)

Burnet, Bishop, *History of His Own Times* (1734)

Burton, J Hill, *History of Scotland* (1873)

Burt's *Letters from the North of Scotland* (1754)

Campbell, Lord Archibald, *The Records of Argyll* (1885)

Campbell, Duncan, *Some Historical Reasons Why Campbell of Glenlyon and the Earl of Breadalbane Hated the MacDonalds of Glencoe* (1912)

Campbell, Duncan, *The Lairds of Glenlyon: Historical Sketches of Appin, Glenlyon and Breadalbane* (1886)

Commission of Enquiry into the Massacre, PRO: King William's Chest 15

Cromartie, Earl of, *A Highland History* (1979)

Dalrymple, Hon Hew, *Genealogical Account of the Dalrymples of Stair* (1909)

Dalrymple, Sir John of Cranstoun, *Memoirs of Great Britain and Ireland 1681–1692* (1771)

Dickinson, W Croft, *Scotland from the Earliest Times to 1603* (Ed A A M Duncan) (1977)

Dundee, Viscount, *Memoirs* (1903)

Drummond, John, *Memoirs of Sir Ewen Cameron of Lochiel* (Ed) (1842)

Fairweather, Barbara. Travellers' Tales from the Highlands (Ed) (1979)

Fairweather, Barbara, *Travels Around Glencoe in Olden Days* (Ed) (1978)

Fyfe, J, *Massacre of Glencoe* (1948)

Gilfillan, George, *Massacre of Glencoe and the Campbells of Glenlyon* (1912)

Gillies, William, *In Famed Breadalbane* (1938)

Glencoe, Massacre. Various MS in National Library: Nos 7014, 3196, 1672, 3735, and 1305

Glencoe, Massacre of. Various editions of Leslie's report (Publ B Bragg 1703 and 1704)

Graham, J M, *Annals and Correspondence of Viscount Stair* (Ed) (1875)

Grant, Dr I F, *Highland Folk Ways* (1961)

Grant, Neil, *The Campbells of Argyll* (1970)

Grimble, Ian, *Clans and Chiefs* (1980)

Highland Papers – see *Maitland Club*

Innes, Cosmo, *The Black Book of Taymouth* (Ed) (1855)

Kincaid, Alexander, *Account of the Depredations Committed on Clan Campbell and Their Followers 1685–1686* (Ed) (1816)

Lamont, Sir Norman, *An Inventory of Lamont Papers* (1914)

Lang, A, *History of Scotland* (1907)

Leslie, Charles, *Gallienus Redivivus, or Murder Will Out . . .* (1720)

Leslie, R J, *Life and Writings of Charles Leslie* (1885)

Linklater, Eric, *The Royal House of Scotland* (1970)

Linklater, Eric, *The Survival of Scotland* (1968)

Linklater, Eric, *The Masks of Purpose* (1957)

Macaulay, Lord, *History of England* (1848)

MacDonald, Revs Angus J and Archibald M, *The Clan Donald 1896–1904*

MacDonald, Donald J, *Clan Donald* (1978)

MacDonald, Donald J, *Slaughter Under Trust* (1965)

MacKechnie, Rev J, *The Dewar Manuscripts* (Ed) (1964)

Mackenzie, A M, *Songs of John MacDonald, Bard of Keppoch* (1964)

Mackie, R L, *Short History of Scotland* (revised) (1962)

Macky, John, *Memoirs of Secret Services* (1733)

Maclean, Fitzroy, *A Concise History of Scotland* (1970)

Maidment, J, *The Argyll Papers 1640–1723* (Ed) (1834)

Maitland Club, *Papers Illustrative of the Political Condition of the Highlands of Scotland 1689–1696* (1845)

Maitland Club, *Memoirs of Hugh Mackay* (1833)

Martin, Martin, *A Description of the Western Islands of Scotland* (reprint) (1934)

Miller, John, *Life and Times of William and Mary* (1974)

Mitchison, Rosalind, *A History of Scotland* (1970)

Moncrieffe, Sir Iain, *The Highland Clans* (1967)

Napier, M, *Memoirs of the Marquis of Montrose* (Ed) (1856)

Petrie, Sir Charles, *The Jacobite Movement* (1959)

Philip, James, *The Grameid. An Heroic Poem Descriptive of the Campaign of Viscount Dundee in 1689* (1887)

Prebble, John, *Glencoe. The Story of the Massacre* (1966)

Ramsay, A A, *The Arrow of Glenlyon* (1930)

Register of the Privy Council of Scotland 1691–1695

Riley, P W J, *King William and the Scottish Politicians* (1979)

Scott, Walter, *The Bride of Lammermoor* (1819)

Scott, Walter, *Tales of a Grandfather* (1830)

Scottish Historical Review. Various vols, including Vols III, XVI, XLVI and XLVII

Skene, W F, *The Highlanders of Scotland* (1837)

Smout, T C, *A History of the Scottish People 1560–1830* (1969)

Somers, J B, *Tracts* (1748)

Stevenson, David, *Alasdair MacColla and the Highland Problem in the 17th Century* (1980)

Van der Zee, H and B, *William and Mary* (1973)

Appendix I:

DESCENDANTS OF THE TWELFTH CHIEFTAIN OF GLENCOE

Alasdair, 12th of Glencoe, murdered 1692

|

John, 13th of Glencoe, died before 1714

|

Alasdair, 14th of Glencoe

|

John, 15th of Glencoe, *floruit* 1785

|

Alexander, 16th of Glencoe, died 1814

|

Ewen, 17th of Glencoe, born 1788, died 1840

|

Ellen Catherine MacDonald, 18th of Glencoe, born 1830, died 1887
(married Archibald Burns, afterwards Burns MacDonald)

Archibald MacDonald,
19th of Glencoe,
died unmarried 1894

Major Duncan MacDonald,
20th of Glencoe,
sold Glencoe 1894

William MacIain MacDonald,
21st Chieftain
died unmarried

Roy Cameron MacDonald,
22nd Chieftain (not
traced since an aircraftman
in RAF in World War II –
unmarried?)

Helen MacDonald,
died 1943
(married Sir Cuthbert
de Hoghton, 12th
Baronet)

Sir Anthony de Hoghton,
13th Baronet
died unmarried 1978

Charles de Hoghton
born 1930, died 1971

Iseult de Hoghton
born and died 1921

Katherine Anne de Hoghton,
born 1959, died 1980

Appendix II:

MUSTER ROLL OF GLENLYON'S COMPANY, QUARTERED IN GLENCOE IN FEBRUARY 1692

Several changes took place within the company before February 1692, including the replacement of Ensign Campbell by Lundie, and of Lieutenant Millon by Lindsay. The question-marks signify illegibility on the original roll.

Muster Roll of Capt Robt Campbell of Glenlyon his Company

Robert Campbell Capt	Robert Barbour Sergent	Mungo Dallzell
John Millon Levt	James Herdrie Sergent	Cuthbert Hunter
John Campbell Ensigne		——Drummers——

Ar(chibal)d Campbell Corp	James Macphell Cor	Dun(can) Kennedie Corp

Ard Gray	Dun(can) MacCallom Er	John Mackechirn
Ard Campbell Er	Dun Macphell	John Stewart
Ard Campbell Yr	Dun MacLawchlane (?)	John Turner
Adam MacCray (?)	Dun Mackunlayroy	John MacCallom
Alex(ande)r Miln	Dun Mackenthor	John Alexander
Ard Blaire	Dun Campbell	Lodvi(c) Robertson
Ard Maclechessag (?)	Dun Robertson	Mall(colm) Sinclair
Ard Morison	Geo(rge) Campbell	Mall MacCallom
Ard Macinkerd	Henry Dyatt	Mall Robertson
Andr(ew) Gray	Jam(es) Campbell	Mall MacClewan
Ard MacLeane	John MacDugald	Morton (?) Mackinbine
Don(ald) Campbell Er	John Dumbar	Niell Gilles
Don Campbell Yr	John Mackenthor	Patt(rick) Mackintyre
Don MacCallom Er	John MacNiellash (?)	Patt Mackechirn
Don MacCallom Yr	Dun Macnachton	Rob(ert) Peatrie
Don MacIvackeder (?)	John Fergusson	Thom(as) Bluntfield
Don MacClewan	John George	Thom Scott
Don Mackunlayroy	Dun MacCallom Yr	Tyrens (?) Obreyan
Don Robertson	John Mackunlay	Walter Tillirey

Stirling, Octob 23rd 1691. Mustered then for Capt Robt Campbell of Glenlyon his Comp for the Earl of Argyll's Regt of Foot — the Capt, Livt, Ensign, two Serjeants, three Corporalls, two Drummers, fiftie seven Sentinells, and this muster is for the months of August, September and October 1691.

Appendix III:

WILLIAM III'S ORDERS OF 16TH JANUARY 1692 TO SIR THOMAS LIVINGSTONE

61. The copy of that paper given in by Mckdonald of Auchterau to Colonell Hill hath been showen to us. Wee did formerly grant passes to Buchan and Canon, and Wee do authorise and allow you to grant passes to them, and for ten servants to each of them, to come freely and safely to Leith, from that to be transported to the Netherlands before the   day of March next, to goe from thence where they please, without any stop or trouble.   2. Wee allow you to receive the submissions of Glengary and these with him, upon their taking the oath of alleagance and delivering up the house of Invergary, to be safe as to their lives, but as to their estates they must depend upon our mercy.   3. Incase you find that the house of Invergary cannot probably be taken in this season of the year, with the artillery and other provisiones that you can bring there, in that case Wee leave it to your discretion to give Glengary the assurance of intire indemnity for life and fortune, upon the delivering of his house and armes, and taking the oath of alleagance. In this you are allowed to act as you find the circumstance of the affair doth require; but it were much better that these who have not taken the benefite of our indemnity in the tearmes, and within the dyet prefixed by our proclamation, they should be obliged to render upon mercy. And the taking of the oath of alleagance is indispensable, others having already taken it.   **4. If M'Kean of Glencoe, and that tribe, can be well separated from the rest, it will be a proper vindication of the publick justice to extirpate that sect of thieves.**

The double of these instructiones are only comunicated to Colonell Hill.

Jan^{ry} 16th, 1692.

INDEX

Achallader, 61, 71, 73, 84, 136, 143
Achnacon, 31, 50, 110, 117, 120
Achtriochtan, 31
Angus Og, Lord of the Isles, 25
Annandale, Earl of, 135
Anne, Queen, 143
Aonach Eagach, 30, 77, 117
Argyll, Colin, 1st Earl, 25, 27
Argyll, Archibald, 5th Earl, 27
Argyll, Archibald, 8th Earl, 43, 45, 46, 48
Argyll, Archibald, 9th Earl, 43, 50, 52, 57
Argyll, Archibald, 10th Earl, 12, 13, 16, 53, 70; military role, 84–90; 95; talks with Stair, 101–103; 107, 108, 111, 112; reactions to massacre, 127–134; 138, 139, 143, 145
Atholl, Marquis of, 52, 58, 59, 108
Atholl raid, 52, 94

Ballachulish, 94, 107, 112, 113, 147
Balloch Castle, 43, 48, 145
Barber, Sgt Robert, 110, 111, 120, 136, 139
Barclay, Sir George, 67, 71, 73, 77
Bidean nam Bian, 31, 33, 77
Black Mount, 28, 32, 97
Breadalbane, John, 1st Earl, 15, 53; rise to power 57–59; 60, 65 negotiations with clans, 70–76; 77 84, 85, 90; talks with Stair, 101–103; 107, 108; reactions to massacre, 127–131; 136, 139, 142, 143, 145
Breadalbane, 2nd Earl, 136, 142
Bruce, Robert I of Scotland, 25
Buchan, Maj-Gen Thomas, 65, 71, 73, 103

Caermarthen, Marquis of, 9
Caithness, Earl of, 57
Cameron of Lochiel, 27, 38, 58, 59, 60, 65, 67, 70, 71, 73, 77, 88, 90, 101, 134
Campbell of Aberuchill, 97
Campbell of Ardkinglas, Sir Colin, 94, 95, 97, 102, 130, 135
Campbells of Argyll, 27, 43, 49, 53, 57, 70, 122; see also Argyll, Earls of
Campbells of Barcaldine, Alexander, 85, 90, 101, 127
Campbell of Carwhin, Colin, 127, 128
Campbell Clan, 13, 16, 25, 39, 43, 45, 46, 48, 49, 50, 52, 84, 85, 94, 111
Campbell, of Dressalch, Colin, 97

Campbell of Glenlyon, 'Mad' Colin, 28, 108 Campbell, of Glenlyon, Robert, 16, 50, 61, reputation, 107–110; 111, 112, 113; actions in Glencoe, 117–120; 122, 127; reactions to massacre, 130–134; 136, 139, 142, 145, 147
Campbell of Glenlyon, John, 145
Campbells of Glenorchy, 26, 43, 48, 49, 57, 73
Campbell of Glenorchy, Colin, 6th Laird, 27
Campbell of Glenorchy, Colin, 8th Laird, 43, 57
Campbell of Glenorchy, Robert, 9th Laird, 46, 48
Campbell of Glenorchy, Sir John, 10th Laird, 108
Campbell of Glenorchy, Sir John, 11th Laird. See Breadalbane
Campbell, Pte James, 120, 135
Campbell, Lady Jean, 108
Campbell, John, 97
Cannon, Colonel Alexander, 60, 61, 65, 67, 103
Carnoch, 31, 49, 50, 94, 110, 117, 145, 147
Charles I, 45
Charles II, 52, 57, 67, 81
Coire Gabhail, 33
Colquhouns of Luss, 28
Cromwell, Oliver, 49, 65, 67, 81

Dalcomera, 58, 59, 73
Dalrymple, Hew, 138, 139
Dalrymple, Sir James, 1st Viscount Stair, 81, 82, 97
Dalrymple, Janet, 81
Dalrymple, Sir John. See Stair, Master of
Devil's Staircase, 30, 113, 120, 122
Don, Duncan, 118
Donald, Clan, 13, 25, 33, 37, 38, 43, 45, 46, 48, 52, 58, 59, 70, 85, 88, 90, 102, 111, 145, 147
Drummond, Capt Thomas, 95, 107, 110, 117, 119, 134, 136, 139
Duncanson, Maj Robert, 84, 107, 111, 112, 113, 117, 120, 122, 130, 131, 136
Dundas, Elizabeth, 82
Dundee, Viscount, 58, 59, 60, 71, 82
Dunkeld, 59, 60, 90

Edward IV of England, 25
Eilean Munde, 38, 123, 145, 147

Finlarig Castle, 48

Forbes of Culloden, Duncan, 134
Forbes, Maj John, of Culloden, 67,
85, 107, 122

Fort William, 46, 48, 65, 67, 76,
84, 85, 88, 94, 95, 101, 103, 106,
107, 108, 110, 111, 112, 113, 120,
127, 130, 134, 147

Gleann-leac-na-muidhe, 31, 50, 110,
122
Glencoe, 12, 13, 16, 17; pattern of
life, 25–39; Montrose wars, 45–50;
53, 58, 61, 65, 73, 77, 94, 97, 102,
106, 107, 108, 110, 111, 112;
massacre, 117–123; 127, 130, 131,
135, 138, 142, 147
Gregor, Clan, 27, 28, 108

Hamilton, Duke of, 135
Hamilton, Lt-Col James, 85, 88,
90, 94, 106, 107, 111, 112, 113,
120, 122, 128, 130, 131, 135, 136,
139
Hill, Col John, 16, 17;
negotiations with clans, 65–70; 76,
77, 84, 85, 94, 95, 97; orders from
Stair, 103–107; 108, 111, 112, 119,
122, 127, 128, 130, 131, 134;
commission of enquiry, 135–139

Inveraray, 43, 46, 50, 90, 94, 95,
97, 107, 130, 134
Inverlochy: see Fort William
Inverrigan, 31, 111, 117, 119, 120,
147

James II, 9, 10, 12, 52, 53, 57, 58,
60, 65, 67, 71, 73, 77, 81, 82, 83,
88, 90, 94, 135
James IV of Scotland, 25
John of the Heather, 25
John of the Isles, 27
Johnston of Wariston, James, 130,
131, 134, 142

Killiecrankie, 59, 65, 73, 82

Lamont, Sir James, 48
Leslie, Charles, 12, 13, 16, 17, 131,
134, 138, 143
Leslie, Gen David, 49
Leven, Loch, 31, 36, 38, 107, 113,
134
Lindsay, Lt John, 107, 108, 110,
117, 118, 136, 139
Linnhe, Loch, 46, 48, 67, 70, 94,
134
Livingstone, Sir Thomas, 16, 65, 83,
84, 85, 101, 102, 103, 106, 111,
112, 128, 130, 135, 139
Lochaber, 25, 32, 67, 84, 90, 101,
103, 134

Lom, Iain, 48, 49, 60
Lordship of the Isles, 25, 27
Lorne, Lord, see Argyll
Louis XIV, 17
Lundie, Ensign John, 110, 117,
136, 139
Lyon, Glen, 49, 50, 108

Macaulay, Lord, 10, 57, 83
MacColla, Alasdair, 45, 46, 48, 49
MacDonald of Achnacon, 110, 120
MacDonald of Achtriochtan, Alexander,
135
MacDonald of Achtriochtan, John, 50,
70, 77, 120, 127
MacDonald, Archibald, 134
MacDonalds of Clanranald, 101, 102
MacDonald of Dalness, Alasdair, 122
MacDonalds of Glencoe, 17, life and
history, 25–39; Montrose wars,
45–49; 50, 53, 60, 61, 71, 76,
84, 95, 97, plans for reprisal,
101–108; 110, 113, 122, massacre
investigation, 127–138; 139, 142
145, 147
MacDonald of Glencoe, John,
8th MacIain, 27
MacDonald of Glencoe, Alasdair,
11th MacIain, 46
MacDonald of Glencoe, Alasdair,
12th MacIain, 12, 16, 46, succession
and early years, 49–53; campaign
with Dundee, 58, 58–61; 65, quarrel
with Breadalbane, 70–73; 77, journey
to Inveraray, 94–97; 102, 103, 106,
107, 108, 110, 113, murder, 118–122;
123, 127, 130, 131, 134, 135, 138,
143, 147
MacDonald of Glencoe, John,
13th MacIain, 50, 52, 58, 107, 108,
110, 117, 118, 119, 127, 134, 135,
145, 147
MacDonald of Glencoe, Alasdair Og,
50, 58, 65, 76, 108, 111, 117,
118, 119, 127, 135, 145
MacDonald of Glencoe, Alasdair,
14th MacIain, 147
MacDonalds of Glengarry, 27, 67, 70,
71, 73, 76, 84, 85, 88, 101, 102,
103, 110, 127, 130, 145
MacDonald of Inverrigan, 110, 119
MacDonalds of Keppoch, 27, 28, 48,
49, 50, 53, 60, 61, 70, 71, 73, 77,
84, 88, 101, 102, 108, 134, 145
MacDonald, Ronald, 120
MacDonald of Sanda, 49
MacDonald of Sleat, Sir James,
50, 52
MacDonnells of Antrim, 45
MacGregors, see Clan Gregor
MacIains of Ardnamurchan, 27
MacIains of Glencoe, see MacDonalds
of Glencoe

Mackay, Gen Hugh, 57, 59, 60, 61, 65, 67, 84, 135
Macky, John, 57
Macleans of Duart, 50, 58, 70, 71, 85, 88, 101
Mary, Queen, 9, 12, 13, 65, 71, 76, 84, 88, 97, 112, 135, 142
Matheson, Murdoch, 123
Melville, Earl of, 70, 83, 85
Menzies, Maj, Duncan of Fornooth, 77, 90
Monck, Gen, 67
Montrose, Marquis of, 45, 46, 48, 49, 57

Namur, fortress of, 17
Newliston, 82, 147
Nottingham, Earl of, 9, 77

Ogilvies of Glenisla, 27

Paris Gazette, 10, 12, 131
Perth, 59, 90
Philip, James, 58
Portland, Earl of, 9, 130
Privy Council of Scotland, 13, 28, 36, 37, 50, 52, 53, 57, 61, 65, 76, 81, 97, 130, 134, 142

Ranald of the Shield, 123

Rannoch Moor, 25, 32, 48, 50, 61, 103
Romney, Earl of, 9
Ross, Earldom of, 25
Russell, Adm William, 9, 12

Signal Rock, 31, 110
Stair, Sir John Dalrymple, Master of, 10, 17, 58, 76, family background, 81–83; 84, plans for reprisal, 85–90; 94, 97, orders for Glencoe, 101–107; 111, 122, 127, reactions to massacre, 128–134; 138, 139, 142, 143, 145
Steinkirk, battle of, 17, 135
Stewarts of Appin, 28, 38, 58, 71, 76, 84, 88, 101, 102, 108, 122, 134
Stuart, Charles Edward, 145

Tay, Loch, 43, 46, 48, 60, 61
Tarbat, Viscount, 58, 70, 76
Tweeddale, Marquis of, 103, 127, 130, 135

William III, King, 9, 10, 12, 13, 16, 17, 53, 57, attitude to Highlands, 65–70; 71, 73, 76, relations with Stair, 81–83; 84, 88, 94, 95, 97, 102, 103, 106, 107, 112, 113, 127, reactions to massacre, 130–143; 145